From Prosecutor to Prison to Preacher

By Billy Gray

Copyright © 2008 by Billy Gray

From Prosecutor to Prison to Preacher
by Billy Gray

Printed in the United States of America

ISBN 978-1-60791-113-5

All rights reserved solely by the author. The author guarantees all contents are original and do not infringe upon the legal rights of any other person or work. No part of this book may be reproduced in any form without the permission of the author. The views expressed in this book are not necessarily those of the publisher.

Unless otherwise indicated, Bible quotations are taken from The King James Version of the Bible.

www.xulonpress.com

ACKNOWLEDGMENTS

From an Estate house to a tiny prison cell to five Continents, God planted, cultivated and molded his servant.

After hearing my testimony, people encouraged me to write a book. This was totally out of my experience and comfort zone.

However, about three years ago I began to write down events as I recalled them about certain sequences in my life. Some recalls were painful and emotionally draining and I would abandon the efforts for weeks or months. But then God would send someone like Marge Pratt to inquire and encourage me.

Reverend David DuVall and wife Amy would critic, make suggestions and remind me God gives us new mercies every morning (Lam. 3:23).

Kathy Edwards a retired copy editor from Life Way put the finishing touches on the manuscript for which I am deeply grateful.

DEDICATION

I dedicate this book to my son, Ty Gray and daughter, Trista Plantholt. They have stood by my side unabashedly through the good times and through the crucibles. And for their devotion and steadfast love, I dedicate this book.

TABLE OF CONTENTS

Chapter 1: The Trial 15

Chapter 2: The Raw Deal 31

Chapter 3: The Sentencing 47

Chapter 4: A New Home 53

Chapter 5: My New Life 65

Chapter 6: My Mentor, "The Preacher" 75

Our Favorite Memory 85

Chapter 7: Coming Home 93

Epilogue 97

FOREWARD

Some thought this book should be titled "An Incredible Journey." From the small wiry boy whose sandy hair knew no discipline to a worldwide missionary. A quantum leap, to say the least.

Born to Walter and Tricie Gray in Memphis, Tennessee, Billy was a gifted athlete, receiving recognition in football, basketball and baseball. He was privileged to go to an elite prep school for four years, Battle Ground Academy. His core values were drawn from his devout Christian parents, as well as from his prep school years.

Graduating from Memphis University Law School in 1964, he began to practice law. Soon thereafter he was selected to serve in the District Attorney General's office and was on staff during the trial of James Earl Ray, the accused murderer of Dr. Martin Luther King. Leaving that position he joined a prestigious law firm with offices in Memphis as well as Washington, DC.

Married to Patricia Derrington, R.N. They had two children, Ty and Trista. Becoming restless, Billy decided to dabble in real estate developments and this is where his life began to unravel.

The intriguing story of how one can fall from the pinnacle to the abyss and still be redeemable is a testimony of God's faithfulness (Rom. 8:28).

Billy said, "I went into prison believing in God and came out knowing Him." To God be the glory!

INTRODUCTION

"The Big house"

I woke up on May 4th, 1978, after a restless night's sleep to a drizzling rain. It was a quiet morning and very few words were exchanged. Pat, Trista and I got into the car. We began a slow drive up the winding pea-gravel driveway. The numerous pecan trees in the front yard of perhaps ten acres were in full bloom. The wetness of the leaves made it appear as though they had been freshly waxed. We arrived at the gated entrance, and I turned to glimpse at the Louisiana Plantation-style home. Columns galore, balconies up and down, stairs on three sides. A "widow's walk" that was prominently displayed against the gray skies. A dream house we all cherished. The thought came to mind that I would never sleep in that house again.

Trista, my five-year-old daughter, was dressed in a bright red raincoat. The shy little child got out of the car, took a few steps, and said, "Bye Poppa." I responded, "Bye, Sweetheart." She took a few more steps and repeated, "Bye Poppa," and waved. It was the last time I would see her for many, many months. I wondered if she understood, in her child-like way, what was in store for her.

CHAPTER ONE

THE TRIAL

It had all begun on a dreary Monday morning. Monday morning, December 13, 1976, was met with a great deal of trepidation, as we walked from the hotel to the Federal Courthouse in Miami, Florida.

As we entered the Courthouse, it was the first time I had experienced security on entering a public building. Most of the courtrooms had been down-sized and modernized. But my trial would be held in a large, ornate, antiquated courtroom with Spanish influence. The metal was highly polished, and the wood appeared freshly attended to. Obviously it was used in high-profile litigation.

The bailiff bellowed, "Hear Ye, Hear Ye," the Honorable James Lawrence King, the One Who Must be Obeyed, asked me, the defendant, to stand. At that time it was the most jarring pronouncement I had ever heard. "The United States of America vs. Billy Gray."

Could this be? All of the people in the United States against me? Was I such a heinous person that gang tackling was necessary? I held on to the table, not trusting my legs to carry this burden.

Prospective jurors were brought in to be "voir dired." Judge King, in his verbose manner, began his litany of our judicial system. What an honor to serve your country as a juror, and it's an awesome responsibility. How he had grown up in South Florida and aspired to the higher ranks of the judiciary. He was puffing like a used car salesman.

Our original judge was Judge Fay, known among the practitioners of the law as fair and balanced. But fate had intervened, and Judge Fay was elevated to the 5th Circuit Court of Appeals. Contrarily, Judge King would lean toward the prosecution's point of view. Not good.

The voir dire began, uneventfully as customary questions were asked. Glen Sisson, my attorney and friend, had some vocal chord problems. Although sartorially attired and his shaven head gleamed as if freshly waxed, the strength of his voice and demeanor was like a balloon that had been stuck with a pin. He became sick before our very eyes.

A recess was called for and granted. We took Sisson to a hospital emergency room. The doctor prescribed bed rest with medication.

Under these circumstances, surely the trial would be continued, but not so with the One Who Must be Obeyed. Judge King's analysis was, important witnesses had been subpoenaed while Congress was on Christmas break, and it would be impossible to have them come back at another time. This would be his time in the spotlight before the dignitaries. Therefore, he would appoint the Public Defender to defend me, and trial would proceed on Tuesday, December 14, 1976.

My faith in the fairness of the judicial system was shaken to the core. The Public Defender protested that he knew very little about my case, and it would not be fair to the defendant to proceed. But proceed we did.

The Public Defender knew what the technical charges were, but nothing about the circumstances that had brought about the indictments. The kind Judge King gave me a couple of hours to explain what had happened and to devise a defense.

"Well, Mr. Public Defender, I am charged with the count of wire fraud and four counts of conspiracy. Originally there was a co-defendant. Unfortunately, he no longer resides on this earth. Without being too complicated, let me give you the story in an aphorism. I was trying to build a project in Belize on Ambergris Caye. My partner had long since grown tired of the snail-paced progress. Trip after trip produced little advancement. My partner, J.D. Rutherford, wanted out.

My personal involvement had become a crusade. The rhapsody of my dream and vision for this quaint little undiscovered piece of paradise impregnated a large part of my thought processes. I was proselytized from lawmaker to a developer in a small, foreign country. To my friends, it was inscrutable. Nevertheless, it was my dream.

Just one problem. I did not have enough money to purchase the land as a sole proprietor. My familiar source for borrowing or raising funds, the bank, was not an avenue available. I needed a visionary whose tentacles reached the venture capitalist. This was no time to capitulate – full throttle ahead! No huddled offense, and the game is on!

Surely with my garish brochures and renderings, one with means would salivate to participate in a project with such promise.

Ambergris Caye is a beautiful little island located in Belize on the Caribbean Sea. A two-hour boat ride from Belize City or a thirty-minute prop flight to the island. The island is approximately seven miles long and averages a half mile wide. The natives had bunched up in a small area, and at that time the population was nearing 1,000. There was only one motor vehicle on the island. All streets are sand-based, no asphalt or concrete. Coconut trees are plenteous as the paths and roads meander through the groves. The water is emerald-green, and on a good day you could see 25 feet down. With the aid of a mask, the most beautiful, colored fish you have ever seen come into view. One mile from shore is the second largest barrier reef in the world. This keeps the water relatively calm near the shoreline, and makes swimming and diving delightful. Some ships have made their final journey trying to cross the reef. Their battered hulls thrash again and again until they dissipate. There are two old houses converted into hotels, and six thatched-roof cabins one shares with the creatures of the island.

Our plans included a desalinization plant, so there would have been adequate drinking and showering water. Otherwise one would have to depend on rainfall water.

Although there were some drawbacks, the good far outweighed the bad. Surely anyone with a Pilgrim spirit would come aboard.

It is surely disappointing when others don't gravitate to your position. But that was the case. Too many "nay-sayers."

That's when I was introduced to Frank Peal, my deceased, indicted co-conspirator. Frank came to me for some small legal matter. He was going to develop a lakeside residential project in Mississippi. As I had done some developing, we had a common bond. Frank had lived in Freeport of the Bahamas for a number of years, and had married a woman from Panama. He liked my idea in Belize, which was of some comfort. The real estate market was not good, and Frank was having trouble getting a development loan as well.

Those who chased the development and investment dollars outside the conventional realm were now introduced to a new source of funding. Oil money. Not only did the oil countries have an abundant supply of money, but they wanted to lend it at high interest rates. Of course, you had to know someone with the "right connection," and for a fee they could plug you in.

A man by the name of Bob O'Neal was introduced to Frank. O'Neal knew a man from the Caribbean who had such a connection and loved my project. For $10,000 he would assure me a loan for $100,000. I took the bait, and he took my money. Time dragged by with no positive results. Daily I was assured, "within the next couple of days all would be well." Like the check in the mail – it never came. Still, being a citizen in good standing, I went to individuals in the FBI who were friends of mine and told them the whole story. The FBI said there was an epidemic of this fraud. I reported to the Caribbean man who was living in Clarksdale, Mississippi, about my visit to the FBI. The next day he sent most of my money back, and then disappeared, never to be heard from again.

Frank and I were furious, and it was time to meet Mr. O'Neal. O'Neal lived near Tupelo, Mississippi, way back in the woods. He gave directions, and Frank's Lincoln driving chauffeur found the house.

Frank Peal was a short man, about 5'4", a paunch for his middle section, and a hair piece. His neck and fingers were decorated with gold and diamonds. His shirt was always unbuttoned so his necklace could be prominently displayed. Frank, in his mid-fifties, dressed as if he still lived in the islands. Colors were bright and loud, grandiose, so to speak. He did not carry his age well, and looked as though he had been "rode hard and put up wet."

Conversely, O'Neal, not sartorially tailored, was groomed in every other aspect of his appearance. He often mentioned that he had his hair trimmed, shaped and combed at the barber shop each day. O'Neal was about 5'10", 175 pounds, with a quick smile and nervous laugh.

It was obvious from the get-go these two men did not like one another. An argument erupted shortly after their initial introduction. It was as if both men were territorial about an armrest on an airplane. Neither would give an inch. Both men were high-strung and volatile and each had had way too much to drink. O'Neal went to the bedroom and came out brandishing a hand gun. O'Neal was furious that his integrity had been challenged. He thought the Caribbean man was on the up and up. He didn't get any of the proceeds. Besides, "I've been to prison before and will go again; I can do time standing on my head."

Peal did not blink an eye or back up. He stood his ground. Now it was his time to vent. I was aghast when Peal stated that he also had spent time in prison, at the Eglin Federal Prison Camp. Undaunted by the pistol, he garrulously labored on the inconsequential.

By now the emotions of both men had been exhausted, and it was time for another drink. The evening ended amicably, and Frank and I rode back to Memphis in silence. He was passed out and I brooded over the strange events. Each man had the compassion of a chainsaw killer and the bedside manner of a drill sergeant. Was it time to dump the dream or pursue it assiduously?

The next morning, early, I sat on the upstairs porch. The temperature was modest, although it was summer. I reviewed the events of the past evening. What strange bedfellows! Having prosecuted and represented cons, crooks and criminals, my intuitive instinct that comes along with the job told me there did not seem to be a measure of decency in these two men. Perhaps now it was time to abandon my dream.

Later on that morning, after arriving at my law office, there was a telephone call from O'Neal. He told me he had a friend in Hollywood, Florida, who had access to large sums of money from an insurance company, and if I would pay the freight, he would like to hear about the project and look at my pro forma. Although tired and exhausted, my adrenalin sent my hopes sky high. My secretary made flight arrangements for Hollywood.

O'Neal drove from Mississippi to the Memphis airport, where I met him. Somehow he looked different. Hair as always in perfect shape, shoes shined and lots of aftershave lotion. He literally beamed as I approached, and commenced immediately to talk incessantly. Part of this was his fear of flying. It was apparent that O'Neal was intelligent but uneducated. For example, he pronounced résumé "re-zoom-ee." During the flight, in my lawyer sort of way, I had a chance to get to know him and let him tell his story as he understood it.

Much of his early life I don't recall, nor did he elaborate, other than indicating it was difficult. In his early teens he heard of a high-stake poker game being played in a cabin in the woods. His plan was to wait until about midnight, when the pots were at their biggest, put on a ski mask and rob the game. It would be dark, and he could run through the woods and easily elude his pursuers. The plan worked like magic. His bag loaded and pockets full, he ran in the dark like a deer to a safe haven.

The next morning, O'Neal came out of a barber shop in a small town in Alabama. I often wondered if his fixation with his hair resulted from his not being able to have timely haircuts as a child. But nevertheless, here he was after a successful robbery, satisfied with his initial entry into big time crime, and it was so easy!

Suddenly a big, black limousine drove up and stopped. Three men who looked like NFL tackles got out of the car. O'Neal's instincts told him something was terribly wrong. His feelings of triumph were immediately transmuted to fear. He was lifted airborne and shoved into the limo. It was a long, quiet ride across state lines, and the destination unknown to O'Neal. It was quite obvious he was out of his league. The three bulky men, one on either side of O'Neal and one facing him, said not a word. He stared into a sky blackened with doubt. His eternal reward could be at hand.

Finally they stopped at a motel on Airline Highway in New Orleans. He was roughly ushered into the presence of a man whom one called Boss.

This petty thief was mesmerized to be on such hallowed grounds of the mafia. He quickly learned that this was a game the Boss had set up, and one didn't mess with the Boss, or, if one did, there would be severe consequences. "Where is the money," he was asked. His body tingled as if stricken by an electric shock. Unable to compose himself, his motor-mouth fired like a machine gun going into diverse directions. The truth of the matter was that O'Neal didn't have all the money. He had had to split the pot with the one who had given him the tip about the game and its location. Some had been spent on new clothes, and of course, the barber, with a very large tip.

For whatever reason, the Boss was impressed with O'Neal's gritty performance and made him a proposition. "Pay back the money now or go to work for me." Unable to pay the money back, O'Neal's decision was never in doubt.

O'Neal's duties, as he explained them, were to collect money for protection from various entities. Loan sharking and robbing high-stakes poker games. Apparently this went on for a number of years.

Ultimately he was convicted of a crime and sent to prison. I never knew what for, or for how long, or where he served. He snitched no one out, and for good behavior was released from the Mafia.

I said, "Wow! "What a story. So what do you do now besides put deals together?" His answer was oblique, and what he did tell me did not yield clarity. O'Neal said he "took down car dealerships." He recently had taken one down in a small Mississippi town. The best I could understand was this: the automobile dealer was in financial trouble, and O'Neal would take over the operation. The floor plan was maximized to the fullest extent, which would increase the inventory. Advertisement was stretched to the limit, and incredible price reductions resulted in lots of sales. The manufacturers were happy and the dealer was not in danger of losing the dealership. There was only one problem. When the car was sold, the money was pocketed and the floor plan was not paid down. So even if the dealership went bankrupt, O'Neal and the owner had plenty of cash.

According to the source, this particular owner had a beautiful wife a show stopper, so to speak. He was desperate to save his business, or walk away with cash. He would sacrifice anything. His wife became part of the deal. She and O'Neal had a secret sexual relationship. The owner became more maudlin; the wife became more addicted to O'Neal's libido. Soon everyone knew. What once was a small sinkhole soon became quicksand, with all parties being engulfed. O'Neal would demand things of her that, before, she would never have contemplated but was now eager to please. It was as if she were a crack cocaine addict.

O'Neal was obtuse, the owner lugubrious, the wife a slut.

When the authorities moved in, O'Neal moved out, pleased with the carnage he left behind. His ego had been massaged.

That was a lot to take in on a two-hour plane ride, as we landed in Ft. Lauderdale for the big meeting.

Mr. X had made arrangements to meet at a Polynesian restaurant in Hollywood, Florida, that evening. I call him "Mr. X" because I'm not sure I ever knew his real name.

He was a short, bland man, nondescript if you will, and Jewish. O'Neal was noncommittal. There was very little small talk, other than I gleaned that X had been to prison for a stock fraud. Of course he was innocent.

X was a matter-of-fact kind of guy, and dived right into the details of my project. Passion was out of the question; this was strictly a numbers game. After looking at my pro forma, it was apparent he had a prodigious grasp of numbers. His questions and insight reminded me of an internal auditor.

Appearing to understand the concept of the development, we moved into the collateral issue.

My proposal was to deed a seven-acre tract of land zoned for a shopping center, valued at $350,000. The land was located in a rapidly growing area, and I was a 50 percent owner. The numbers made sense to X. Collateral of $175,000 for a $100,000 loan. I was instructed to come by X's office the next morning and pick up the check.

Back at the hotel, O'Neal could not help but boast about his connections and what a financial genius X was.

The next morning X came by the hotel and delivered the $100,000 check, stating that he had forgotten about a mandatory board meeting.

The check was made out to me, drawn on an insurance company. I thanked X and told him we both had a great deal, while O'Neal erupted in pure joy.

Our emotions drained, the flight back to Memphis was in solitude. I bid O'Neal farewell at the airport, never expecting to see him again. Good riddance.

The next morning I went to see Jo Monday, my friend and banker at the 1st National Bank in Germantown, Tennessee. I deposited the $100,000 check, and Joe offered to give me immediate credit. I told him, "No, let's make sure it clears first."

The peace that passes all understanding was not part of my disposition. Our emotions, the least trustworthy of all our senses, left me flummoxed.

At my office, a search was made of the insurance company which issued the check. There was a large insurance company in California by that name, but not in Florida.

The whole thing began to smell to high heavens, like a four-day-old dead rat in your attic.

Two weeks passed, and Joe Monday called and said, "There is no such account." So much of my time had been consumed with my passion that I had neglected my law practice and had spent several thousands of dollars chasing a broken dream.

My pride wounded, it was time to retaliate with a vengeance. Not knowing how to get in touch with X, I called O'Neal. "O'Neal, you and whatever his name is are going to jail." There was stunned silence on the other end. Then a stuttering O'Neal pleaded for time to rectify this egregious error.

That night O'Neal called me at home and said X had been called back to the home office in California. The insurance company had not yet received its permits to operate in Florida; therefore, all operations had been suspended until such time as approvals were granted. O'Neal had recaptured his swagger, and it was time for the bait. X would meet us in San Francisco, "and we'll put this baby to bed."

As fools rush in, O'Neal and I were on a plane to San Francisco. At my expense, of course.

It was July 1975, and San Francisco was cold after coming from the heat and humidity in Memphis. We went to an elegant hotel in the downtown district, where I had arranged a suite for us.

After checking in, it was early evening and the summit would soon begin. X, the bland little balding man with an expressionless face, began his defense. It was all a corporate error, and the company had been too anxious to start its operations in Florida. It had caused him much pain and embarrassment, and he was left with no alternative other than to resign his position.

I was blown away with the tactic, marveling at his ingenuity. This man's heart and soul were impenetrable.

X's monotone voice began to get on my nerves. My stoic disposition was becoming unraveled.. But instead of lashing out, I tried to appeal to this heartless man, recounting all the travails I had been through with Peal, O'Neal, the black man from Mississippi and, of course, X himself. I delayed in playing my trump card of the fraudulent check to see where X would go next.

Mr. Monotone would come to his own rescue. He had thought long and hard about my dilemma and innumerable attempts to obtain financing. And, using his vast source of financial contacts, he had found a private financier who was very interested in Caribbean properties. He gave me the name and number of an individual in Miami, Florida.

We shook hands and X disappeared, never to be heard from again.

I shared the name and number of the new contact with no one. As the Blessed Virgin Mary, I pondered these things in my heart. It was frustrating to some extent. My head said "no," but my heart said "yes," as to whether to act on this new information.

Several days passed, and Peal visited my law office unexpectedly. I invited him to lunch at the Petroleum Club. The Club was then located on the mezzanine of the old, famous Hotel Peabody in downtown Memphis. Only men could enter the dining room and bar facilities at lunch time. The waiters were all black and formally attired.

I often wondered how many deals of gigantic proportion had been made over the years at this club. The setting was formal, but conducive to doing business. My placid exterior was still intact, but my insides were like an ancient city with broken-down walls.

I opted for a martini lunch to keep from hyperventilating. Peal had his usual: half gin and half vodka on the rocks.

Peal, being pushy and inquisitive, started pressing for details and the latest developments on my loan acquisition.

Alcohol usually produces loose lips, and this was true in my case. My thought process was, what better place to examine a potential scam than with the Doctor of Con, Peal.

A cursory report was given about the trip and its results to Hollywood, Florida. Then a more detailed description about the visit to San Francisco.

Peal immediately blamed O'Neal as he aired his acrimonious feelings. It reminded me of two barracudas in the same tank. One would kill the other for the high prize. The high prize in this case was money.

As we continued to drink, Peal's curiosity about this unknown benefactor was magnified.

We left the Club and drove to his plush office in East Memphis. His office was colorfully decorated. Well laid out, with an artist's touch. Relaxing, and the latest electronic equipment, along with a well-stocked bar.

On the first floor of the office building was a bank. Peal called a lady bank official to come up and act as our barmaid.

We continued to drink and discuss the pros and cons about calling the Miami number.

Never having been a really open person, I was somewhat reluctant to discuss business in front of a woman I'd never met. Peal assured me she was all right. She had a key to his safety deposit box, where he kept large sums of cash, jewelry and other items he held safe from creditors and the IRS.

Day gave way to nightfall, and a decision was made. I rang the number in Miami. It was a Mr. Ponsdolt. I introduced myself and told him who had given me his number. We spoke at length about Caribbean properties. He was far more knowledgeable than I about the area, other than my coveted piece of property. He gave me the impression the amount of money we were talking about was inconsequential. We discussed collateral, pay-back methods and interest.

It was a very run-of-the-mill business conversation. And then came, "Oh, by the way."

Ponsdolt then launched into a tirade about some man in Memphis who had accused him of fraud in a stock transaction. Because of this he was being investigated by the Justice Department and an indictment was imminent. Therefore, the funds he had would not be readily available, as they may have to be used for defense purposes. On the other hand, if I could intervene, the money would be available immediately.

I was like a sailboat with a brisk breeze against the sails, and all of a sudden there is no wind.

My response was that ordinarily this was not a type of criminal case in my bailiwick, but if he would send me the papers and charges, I would look at them and give him an opinion.

After hanging up the phone, Peal, in a drunken stupor, jumped for joy. "Now we got it, we got a pigeon and both of our projects will be funded." Not fully understanding Peal's mind-set, I didn't know how to respond.

Peal, as though dipped into a "sober" barrel, began to calculate his approach. He would call the SOB and tell him what a great lawyer I was, how politically connected, and that I could work magic within the framework of the law that would make Houdini proud. You could see the hubris disposition in the squinty eyes of this little despot.

My head was reeling; things were moving too fast. It was like when you were a child, riding on the merry-go-round, reaching for the brass ring to get a free ride. But as you approached the ring, it would whiz by and you would be empty-handed and broken-hearted. I went to the bathroom.

When I returned, Peal was on the phone talking in a loud, vulgar voice. He was calling the names of senators – Erwin, Baker, Brock, Eastland and Stennis. I asked the banker-turned-barmaid who he was talking with. She exclaimed, "The same man you were!" Peal ended the conversation with, "Okay, my friend. Just rest assured that he can fix your case."

I exploded, and admonished Peal never to use the word "fix" in my presence, or associated with my name.

The next morning, with a groggy mind and hung-over, I dialed the Miami number and left a message that "fixing cases" was not part of my repertoire. In my mind this concluded the matter.

Dodging Peal's persistent phone calls and pressure, it was time to return to a normal life of practicing law and taking care of family. However, I had promised my son Ty a trip to Belize before he started back to school. In early August, 1975, the two of us flew to Belize and then over to the island, Ambergris Caye.

Ty and Trista

Ty was mesmerized by the thatched huts, emerald green waters and sand streets. By this time, I was well known on the Caye and had the status of a folk hero. The people treated Ty with the same reverence.

Having legal matters to take care of in the States, I left Ty on the island with friends and would return with his mother, Pat, in one week.

Pat picked me up at the Memphis airport and said there was a man in Miami who was desperately trying to get in touch with me. After arriving at the office, my secretary, Wanzor, said there was an urgent message from Mr. Ponsdolt. On my desk was unopened correspondence, a copy of the indictment of Ponsdolt among them. I read the indictment carefully, digesting the most minute detail. Enclosed with the indictment were two newspaper articles about Ponsdolt from New Jersey, and what he was charged with. It seemed as though he had a history of fraudulent activities. Included in the newspaper articles was a picture of Ponsdolt: a well-dressed man with pleasant features.

The urgent message had a New Jersey area code. Hesitantly, I dialed the number. On the receiving end, a person who identified himself as Ponsdolt answered the phone. I was not sure. He spoke as if he were in a hurry and excited. The voice of the man with whom I had spoken before was very even, with measured tones. The end result was that he wanted me to come to New Jersey, sign on to take his case, and pick up the $100,000 in cash. I told him there were legal matters for me to take care of at home, and in a week my wife and I would be flying to Belize to pick up my son. Coming to New Jersey was out of the question. That was the end of the conversation.

CHAPTER TWO

THE RAW DEAL

The next day Ponsdolt called again, and asked for my flight schedule to Belize. He now wanted to meet me in Miami. He gave me an alias to use when buying my airline ticket and he had reserved a room in that name for the hotel in the airport. This was, according to him, because the loan was a cash transaction.

I gathered the documents to be used as collateral while Pat packed our suitcases, Wearing a yellow suit, which was very fashionable at that time, I purchased two First Class tickets to Miami in my own name. All Pat knew was that there was a potential lender in Miami to buy the Belize property.

Along with my documents were the indictment and the two newspaper articles. Not having met Ponsdolt, I familiarized myself with his photograph in the newspaper.

After exiting the plane, we made our way to the hotel. Using the alias at the front desk, we were given a key and did not have to register. That was strange. When we entered the room, it held just a couple of chairs and a desk. Perhaps this was a room just for business meetings, I thought. Soon there was a knock at the door. A man came in and introduced himself as Ponsdolt. I immediately knew this was not Ponsdolt, even if the newspaper photo was not a good one.

Not even close. His coat was not well-tailored; you could see the impression of a sidearm. Sometimes when you become frightened, you become more stoic. Who was this man? My mind started zig-zagging like a water bug on a pond. Could this be the Mafia?

My first thought was to get Pat out of that room. If harm was coming to me, so be it, but not her. Pat was asked to leave the room and go to the gift shop while we discussed business. After her exit, the imposter said he had the cash downstairs and did I want to see it? I said, "No, we have other business to discuss, like the collateral, the note and the indictment. Besides," I said, "it would not be safe to take $100,000 in cash out of the country." This was not persuasive to the imposter. He insisted we go get the money. I was likewise steadfast in my refusal.

Suddenly the side door was banged open and two or three men with drawn guns identified themselves as the FBI and I was under arrest.

Taken downtown to the FBI headquarters, I was drilled for information. The old system of good cop/bad cop was clearly on display. Most of the questions were about Peal. They evidently knew more about him than I did. If only a confession was given, they would go light on me. "After all, we know that Peal is the bad guy."

Being a former prosecutor, I knew this scene well. If the situation had not been so serious, it would have been amusing. What was I supposed to confess to? What crime had I committed? What had Peal done that I didn't know about?

A decision had to be made instantly, either to talk and trust the FBI or abide by Miranda rights and remain silent. My past experiences with the FBI as a prosecutor tilted my choice to remain silent. This infuriated the bad cop. He imploded by saying, "You will be in prison until you are an old man."

Convinced that they could not inveigle me into making a statement, they took me to the Dade County jail. This was truly a frightening experience. The jail was over-crowded; the prisoners were uncomfortable, and some confused. Shouting and screaming at I don't know what! Most seemed to be of Spanish descent that came from a plebeian society. Still dressed in a yellow suit in contrast to the other guests, a plethora of fear gripped my innermost being. Gratefully, the jailer recognized this would be a very unsafe place for me and decided to place me in the back of the jail, away from the other prisoners. This was the women's jail cells, and they were unoccupied. My best recollection is that all that was in the cell was a concrete floor and bars. Nothing to sit on.

My thought processes kicked into gear about what was happening. I learned from the FBI that Peal was supposed to come to Miami the next day. Apparently there had been conversations to which I was not privy. The FBI was going to set him up as they had me. This could be a dangerous thing. Peal could either set me free or sell his soul by cooperating and bury me. There was no question in my mind which course he would choose. Not knowing how to get in touch with Pat, how was I to best use my one phone call? Over the years, in visiting Ambergris Caye, I had met a woman who lived in Ft. Lauderdale. Although late, I called. When she answered the phone, it was obvious a party was going on. She seemed happy to hear from me, and wanted to talk. "There is very limited time to talk," I stated to her without revealing my whereabouts or situation.

"Call this number," which was Peal's, "and tell him not to come to Miami. It's a trap. Say nothing more and hang up." She promised she would. I felt like Peal's phone was tapped, and it would be a critical error on my part to call and warn him.

The usual Federal procedure would be for me to appear before a magistrate the next morning for a bond hearing. The

FBI, in its kindness, must have told Pat that. Later on that night she appeared with a bail bondsman. I was called up and talked with them via phone. The bail bondsman informed me bond would be set at a $25,000 secured bond. Pat was instructed to take the deed on our home and use it as collateral, but wait until we heard what the magistrate had to say.

It was a long, cold night. Keeping the jail cold is done on purpose, especially when overcrowded. Tempers do not flare as much, and nervous energy is used to keep one warmer. I huddled in a corner on the floor, my teeth chattering and my body shaking as though I had palsy.

Around 9:00 a.m. the FBI escorted me to the Federal Building. Preliminary hearings are held in a smaller courtroom not nearly as ostentatious. I spotted Pat at once, and thought how beautiful she was. Fresh, clean and pure. Seated beside her was the rotund bail bondsman, looking as though he was ready for dessert — money, that is. One of the bailiffs kindly told me I had messed in my britches. It clearly was showing through my yellow suit pants. I took my yellow coat off and tied it around my waist, being deeply embarrassed. The Assistant U. S. Attorney came over and introduced himself. It made me feel like the person the world had known me as 14 hours earlier. He said, "I didn't know you were a fellow attorney; therefore, I'm going to request you be released on your own recognizance." In other words, no secured bond. I looked back at the rotund bail bondsman, who had a grin on his face like a Cheshire Cat who had spotted a mouse, and gave a wink to Pat with a thumbs-up. She did not know the relevance of the gesture at that time. The magistrate took the bench.

I still did not know what the charges were. Then it was announced; the government had accused me of conspiracy and extortion. I almost messed my pants again. The Assistant U. S. Attorney spoke and informed the court that in his opinion the defendant should be released on his own recognizance but confined to the jurisdiction of southern Florida and the State of Tennessee. I heard a rustle in the back of the courtroom. It was the rotund bail bondsman leaving in a huff. No dessert today. The judge agreed. But there was still one problem. Should I be so bold as to address the matter? Playing on house money, could I lose it all with my request? Someone accused of "serious crimes" asking to leave the country the very next day? Pat had never been out of the country on her own. She would have a difficult time with primitive people and their idiosyncrasies. I spoke up and told the judge we were on our way to Belize to pick up our 15-year-old son. We had no other provisions for him. The judge listened sympathetically and looked for guidance from the Assistant U. S. Attorney. There was no objection, and he enlarged my jurisdiction to include asking for permission in the future if I were leaving the country. Pat and I walked out arm in arm. This would be our last legal victory.

After spending a few days on the island, we, as a family, prepared to come home. I walked the island alone, as I awoke to my last summer dawn on this piece of paradise, recounting all of the trips to the island, remembering all of the people who had been introduced to Central America. The song "Land of Broken Dreams" resonated in my mind. It was over now. Defeat had been accepted.

We had talked to no one in Memphis, and therefore had no idea what reception we would receive on our return. Pat, with her social friends? My professional friends? Ty's classmates? Church family and personal family?

Much to our delight, nothing had changed, at least not spoken in our presence.

Early the next morning I was awakened from a deep slumber by the annoying ring of the telephone. "Billy, have you seen the paper?" "No, I'm still in bed." "Go get the newspaper. They have dismissed the indictments."

Jumping out of bed on the second floor, I ran downstairs and out the door, raced down the winding pea gravel driveway to the mailbox and retrieved the Commercial Appeal. It was a small article, hard to find, but headlines to me, stating the indictment had been dismissed "Without Prejudice." My emotions didn't soar to high because of the words "without prejudice." I decided to be mum about the legal technicality and treat it as a victory for family's and friends' sake. However, I knew deep in my heart that the government had one year to reinstitute the charges before the Statute of Limitations expired.

That morning, outside of criminal court, lawyers of all practices congratulated me with warm hearts. The criminal court judges were equally as enthusiastic.

But life did not go on as before. My law partner decided to become an Assistant District Attorney in another county, and moved. My practice was moved to another location, and my relationship with the lawyers with whom I shared space was cordial but not warm. Being cynical of law enforcement's investigation in criminal cases, they were challenged on each point. This was certainly a departure from the past. Many law enforcement people had been cultivated as friends from the days of being a prosecutor. Many came to me for legal advice.

My intentions were to be upbeat at all times with family and friends. If people knew deep down there was a change, it was not brought to my attention. Drinking more and earlier became part of my modus operandi, along with seclusion.

Sometime during this year, I was called and told that Peal was dead. The story goes that Peal and a business partner and his wife were fishing in Grenda Lake in Mississippi. A disturbance came up and the boat and its occupants were in trouble. The boat capsized. It was explained that Peal either drowned or had a heart attack, but nevertheless he was dead in the water. His partner drowned, and his wife swam safely to shore.

A glimmer of hope was restored as to the conclusion of the matter. Not knowing what the government proof would be, surely they would need Peal's testimony to convict me.

While in Florida celebrating our 15th wedding anniversary on August 26, 1976, and one day before the Statute of Limitations expired, I was informed that an indictment had been secured by information. The charge, wire fraud and 5 counts of conspiracy. Arraignment was set for October 7, 1976, in the Federal Building in Memphis, before the Honorable Aaron Brown. A $20,000 secured bond was requested.

With the exception of my five-year-old daughter Trish, the burden to bear was heavy for the entire family. We drove back to Memphis in solitude.

It was now time to dig deep. To put on war paint and man the trenches. To hire a lawyer in Memphis or Miami? To spend huge resources on a defense, or, if things didn't go well, leave my family fairly well off? It was a time of trepidation.

I called my friend Glen Sisson to make an appointment. We sat down and I explained the story as I understood it. Other lawyers were consulted. It was the general consensus that the government didn't have much of a case, especially since Peal was dead.

It was decided that Sisson would represent me and begin to collect evidence from the government. We would have to move fast, for the trial date was set for November 8, 1976.

As scheduled, on October 7, 1976, I appeared before Judge Brown for an assignment and pled not guilty. Judge King, of Miami, requested a surety bond for $20,000. Judge Brown, knowing me, set an unsecured bond and I was released. It was now time to give all of my energy and efforts toward a defense. The date was rapidly approaching.

While the defense team was scurrying around to solidify a defense, I returned to my roots. Raised in a conservative Southern Baptist background, I prayed often and profusely. Although we attended church frequently, taught classes and gave financially, I could not abandon the rudder of my life. For the first time since my youth, people in the church became more than acquaintances, and became friends. They reached out and loved us in a special way. Ten men were nominated for deacon to fill four vacancies. I came in fifth. This outpouring of love and concern was overwhelming.

As each pretrial motion was filed, each was rubber-stamped, "Denied."

Absolutely no one could figure out why this case was being prosecuted. Who had a vendetta against me and for what reason? Was it because of the high-profile senators? No money exchanged hands. I had not spoken with anyone in authority about Ponsdolt and his case. What was the big deal?

Late one evening, Sisson, David Bales, a young lawyer who was observing my case, and I were strategizing about the case. Sisson suggested he call the U. S. Attorney's office and see if they were amenable to a plea of guilty to a misdemeanor. His reasoning was that there would most likely be no prison time and I would not lose my law license. I was not keen on the idea, but allowed the call to be made. The U. S. Attorney's office told Sisson they had explored that idea, and would gladly do it, but the charges as they were could not be reduced to a misdemeanor. For the first time, I saw a crack in the armor of confidence in the defense team.

Sisson, Bales and I boarded a plane on Sunday morning, December 12, 1976. The trial would commence the next day. The lawyers were in a gala mood, telling jokes and drinking whiskey. This disturbed me; didn't they know that my life was on the line? My reputation? My law practice? I was quiet and sullen.

Other witnesses would come as the trial proceeded, including Pat.

"Well, Mr. Public Defender, that's my story." "That's too much to be comprehended in such short order," he said. But Judge King was obstinate; the trial must go forward, if for no other reason than to accommodate the elected officials.

Marsha Lyons, the prosecutor, began to call her witnesses. The lady banker-turned-bartender testified that she had overheard the conversation between me and Peal plus someone in Miami. She stated it was about land and money; that Peal had stated that I could help him with his case if the money was right. I realized immediately that this was the only evidence they had that could place me with Peal on the ill-fated night of the call.

Before the trial, the FBI had called me in Memphis to do a voice print. The purpose for this procedure is to match the voice with the voice on the wire tap from the conversation with Ponsdolt. Their conclusion was that there were some similarities but not a positive ID. Therefore, without the banker-turned-bartender, there was no case. My attorney asked no questions.

A man from the telephone company was called to verify that on the night in question there were three phone calls made from Peal's phone in Memphis to Ponsdolt's phone in Miami. I knew of two of these, but not the third. It was made after I had left that night. Again, no questions.

As I reviewed the prosecution's case thus far in my mind, it went something like this: Peal and I had spoken to someone in Miami about land and money. A telephone person said three calls had been made from Peal's phone to Miami the night in question. Now the question begs, how do you introduce the taped conversation without permission from the court? The public defender rose to address the matter when the prosecutor introduced the taped conversation into evidence. "Do you have a warrant?" "No." "Isn't there a state statute that prevents wire tapping without a warrant?" 'Yes, but I would like to introduce into evidence a statement from the Attorney General's office for the State of Florida that states they will waive the enforcement of the statute in this case."

You talk about a quantum leap! It makes odious seem saintly! Of course, the One Who must Be Obeyed ruled in favor of the prosecution.

The prosecutor informed all parties that the tapes were approximately three hours long. Judge King indicated that he had not heard the tapes, but would rule on their admissibility if any objections were lodged during the playing of same before the jury.

"Oh, by the way," said Judge King. "I have other duties to perform while the tapes are being played. There are a number of Haitians that must be sworn in. In my absence, Ms. Lyons will be in charge. If there are any questions, stop the tape and have the bailiff fetch me. I will come back in the courtroom and make a ruling as to admissibility."

This was a harbinger of our low standing before the court. I felt like a wounded gazelle with a tiger on my tail. My new defense attorney, the Public Defender, was aghast! Stunned into submission, the tapes were entered into evidence and began to play.

Being a student of "reading" jurors, they appeared to exhibit an astute interest. I whispered to the P.D., "This could be the ball game." He nodded in the affirmative.

Most of the tapes were Peal talking to Ponsdolt. Peal was loud, vulgar and garrulous. His words were slurred from too much alcohol, and laced with profanity. Not only did it make me cringe, but it clearly embarrassed the women on the jury. There was no one to identify who was speaking. The jury had never heard me speak. God forbid, did they think this trash-talking irascible person was me?

The P.D. made an objection. The tape was stopped. The judge was called back into the courtroom. "Irritated" might best describe his demeanor. It was akin to someone getting a phone call after they had fallen asleep. The objection was well made, and for a moment, just a moment, it appeared the judge might rule in our favor.

Ms. Lyons was startled. She could see her case crumbling like ice cream melting on a hot summer's day. She resorted to the age-old feminine technique. Her lips puckered, voice trembled with emotion and tears ran down her cheeks. Well, this was too much for the manhood of the judge, and he ruled in her favor.

It seemed as if the tapes went on for an eternity. Like sitting in a dentist's chair as he drills and hits a raw nerve.

Finally the torture was over. Everyone — counsel, jury, defendant and all witnesses — was exhausted. It was a turning point in the case. The prosecution had laid their cornerstone of evidence. It was my opinion this was an epiphany for the jury.

The next day was not an improvement. Ponsdolt, whom I had never met but immediately recognized from newspaper articles with pictures, testified to the phone calls and the caller who identified himself as Billy Gray. He stated he could not identify Gray because he had never met with him. The conversation was about a loan for assisting with a criminal indictment. It was Peal, he stated, who indicated Gray had enormous influence with the senators and other public figures. It was evident that Ponsdolt was shrewd and knew his way around in legal proceedings. At the time, we didn't know why he was so skilled, as we knew little about his background. Speaking in measured tones, he was an effective witness.

No cross examination.

The FBI agent took the stand. He was the imposter for Ponsdolt. His testimony was that the FBI had observed Pat and me board the plan in Memphis. They followed us from the plane's departure to registration at the hotel. He then gave a vivid description of the arrest.

Having participated in many trials with FBI agents, I would have ranked him as only fair-to-middlin'. But untrained civilians think their word (the FBI) is immutable. The expressions on the faces of the jurors told the whole story.

I remember in the early part of my prosecution career, the star witness in the State's case was an agent of the FBI. A burglary case that spread throughout many states, and as an interstate transgression, the FBI became involved. The suspect was arrested at the Rivermont Hotel during the course of a heist in Memphis. He previously had been arrested by the FBI agent in another state. Bond was set; defendant disappeared and had been on the lam now for several years when he fell into the hands of the Memphis Police Department.

The FBI had egg on its face and wanted to ensure a conviction. Therefore, although not necessary for a conviction, the federal agent would testify as to the multiplicity of burglaries.

The agent informed me right before trial he would not be able to identify the defendant. Too many years had passed since he last saw him. I assured the agent that his identification was inconsequential, since we had other police officers who could and would identify the defendant.

I called the agent to the stand and asked the routine question, "Can you describe the defendant and do you recognize him?" Much to my amazement, he answered, "Yes." I was taken aback since only minutes before he had told me he would not recognize the defendant. Chevrolet®, apple pie and the FBI were the proud traditions of America's honesty and goodness. My esteem for the FBI had been diminished. How many convictions had been wrought over the years from lying testimony?

It was now pile-on time, as the government would parade their star witnesses one after another until the emotions reached a grand crescendo. It was orchestrated that well. Basically, each of the star-studded witnesses would testify that they had never talked with me concerning the Ponsdolt matter. It wasn't so much their testimony as it was the pomp and the ceremonial fashion in which each was called to the witness stand.

The calling of the two Tennessee Senators, Howard Baker and Bill Brock, was rather routine and normal. No elaborate introduction, just systematic legal procedure. Name, address, position (United States Senator), and did you ever talk with the defendant (Billy Gray) about a pending criminal case. No.

As I sat at the counsel table, writing pleading prayers, the momentum had drastically shifted. I felt as though I was observing a dying man gasping for his last breath. My mind flashed back to when I was a prosecutor. When you had the defendant on the run, never, ever let up. Like a jackhammer, keep drilling until there is no resistance.

In Little League through Junior High School, you would always put the worst athlete in right field. Then you would pray that no balls would be hit to him, and furthermore he would not come to bat when it was consequential. In other words, don't depend on him when the game is on the line.

That's the way I felt about my newly appointed attorney. A kind, considerate man, but no belly for a fight. In the courtroom, he was a Junior High right fielder.

You could almost hear the drum rolls as Senator James Eastland was called to the stand. A large man with an imposing figure. We were all shocked when Judge King shot out of his chair in an upright position, as though he was in the presence of royalty. He leaned over the bench and grasped Senator Eastland's hand. He then commenced a homily on the importance of this man and the committees he chaired in the Senate, emphasizing, no less, that he chaired the Judicial Committee which appointed and/or approved all federal judges.

Lordy, mercy. Were we going to have a trial or a hanging? Finally my attorney conjured up enough courage to make an objection. "Your Honor, I believe extolling the witness's laudatory position is detrimental to my client." The judge responded, "Perhaps you're right, counselor. Jury, please disregard any remarks that I have made about the distinguished Senator. Proceed, Ms. Lyons."

We had no questions, and for all practical purposes the game was over and the jury would not disregard the judge's comments.

While we were still struggling to catch our breath, the government called the "Old Country Lawyer from South Carolina, Sam Erwin." Of course, everybody knew him from the Nixon hearings and frequent appearances on TV. He was a large man, dressed in a typical Washington business suit. Jowls that reminded me of Winston Churchill were prevalent, and complemented by his megaphone voice. Same testimony, same results. No questions.

When the day ended and court was adjourned, I was like a wet noodle.

Pat flew down for the last day of the trial. My evening facade was a pretense of confidence fueled by large amounts of alcohol.

The next morning, arising early, I stepped out on the balcony of the hotel room. Inhaling deeply from the cigarette, I watched the sunbeams dance across the calm waters of the Atlantic Ocean. A power boat raced towards its destination. A sailboat seemed content to move at a leisurely pace, with the water lapping against its hull. It was peaceful. Suddenly I was jolted back to reality. The uninvited battle of Armageddon had encroached on my peaceful posture, and reality had once again set in.

Not many spectators in court this day. The old-timers know when a rout is on. Jimmy Neal, a Watergate attorney from Nashville, would testify. A congressman's son and other incidental witnesses, and the government would conclude its case. The prosecution smelled blood and the aroma was pleasant.

The court adjourned until the next day. It was now the defense's turn at bat.

That afternoon the newly-appointed lawyer wanted to go over the details once again. There was still a great deal of ambiguity in his mind about this case.

CHAPTER THREE

THE SENTENCING

The next day in court, Sisson decided he was well enough to join the fray. I chose to take the stand in my own defense.

Our first witness was an old, trusted friend, John Davis. John testified that I had called him the night of the alleged calls to Ponsdolt and asked him to come to Peal's office and pick me up. He stated that I had been drinking that afternoon with Peal, and did not feel comfortable driving home. He further testified he spent about an hour in the office with "Billy and Peal" and then drove me home. There were no telephone calls made in his presence.

The next witness was a very prominent businessman from Memphis, Lawson Newman. He was a character witness, and his testimony under normal conditions would have boded well. But it was now December 23rd, and sugar plums were dancing in the heads of some jurors.

Pat testified that I was a good and loyal husband. Her testimony brought tears to my eyes, not from what she said but for what she was going through. They did cross-examine her as to what she knew about the case, which was nothing.

Then the moment everyone was waiting for came. The defendant, Billy Gray, rose, was sworn in and took the witness stand. Sisson was back at the counsel table, and he would be in charge of the direct examination. He lobbed softball questions, and each time I would hit it out of the park.

Basically, our defense was that this was a legitimate business deal and was not about "fixing" a case. With Peal's intrusion, it cast a dark shadow over an ordinary business deal. We proffered a written note between Ponsdolt and myself that met all the legal criteria. The note was for $100,000. Attached to the note was my collateral, a piece of property in which my interest was worth several hundred thousands of dollars.

The question was asked, "Why did you go to Ponsdolt instead of a bank?" My reply: "I was told by O'Neal and his source that Ponsdolt often lent money on Caribbean properties and banks were not interested in collateral outside of the United States."

The rest of direct testimony was more or less about the good things I had done. Church, working with alcoholics, and so forth.

It was now the government's time to annihilate the defendant. Ms. Lyons came out like a roaring lion. I must admit I was a savvy veteran in courtroom procedure and the roaring lioness became a sardonic lamb.

There was no elegance in this courtroom procedure on either side.

Closing arguments were elephantine. Long, laborious and uninspired. There would be no converts.

The judge gave a long, rambling charge to the jury, seemingly heavily weighted in the government's favor.

After about three hours, the jury came back to ask a question. Judge King reminded them it was close to Christmas (then December 23rd, 1976), so a quick decision was in order. Mentally, I could hear the musical instruments line up, for the Fat Lady was about to sing.

One hour later, the jury came back. Guilty on all but one count.

When Joseph was traveling to check on his brothers at his father's request, he had no idea what was in store for him. Perhaps he was a little narcissistic, with his coat of many colors. Maybe he thought his brothers would be glad to see him. But the flaunting of the garment would prove to be a grievous miscalculation.

In one brief moment, I had crossed the line of respectability to a convicted felon. Had I been too full of hubris in the approach to the trial? Should we have filed a motion to have the trial moved to Memphis? Did I choose the right attorneys?

Joseph might have asked, "Why me, God? I'm not such a bad guy." Those were precisely my thoughts.

The lawyers and I tried to be brave in front of Pat. "There are more holes and errors in the trial than in a used pair of underwear." I orally agreed, but deep in my heart, I knew there were stormy days ahead.

Christmas came and went, and to the public our lifestyle had not changed. Most people thought that this was just a bad dream that ultimately would have a different conclusion.

In January, the piercing truth shattered my hope when the Tennessee Bar told me to wind up my practice as soon as possible and surrender my license. If indeed the conviction was upheld on appeal, then I would be disbarred. This was a stinging defeat emotionally. I knew God had given me the talent to be a trial lawyer, and now I had blown it.

As the children of Israel being held captive in Egypt begged, cried and pleaded to no avail, then God sent his servant Moses to lead them out. That was my prayer. "Oh, God, send me a Moses." "How long, oh Lord, how long?" There was not a day that went by for the next year and a half that my emotions would not have huge mood swings. How would my family survive, both financially and emotionally? How was I going to make a living? Every day pleading and praying...

That year and a half may have been the toughest of my life. Commencing the days with hope, ending them in despair, emotionally up and down, but a stoic front for the public and family.

After a motion for a new trial and other legal proceedings, it was now time for me to stand before Judge King for sentencing. We had received a copy of the presentencing investigation. They had recommended a probated sentence, or a minimal sentence of a few months. The prosecution recommended six months incarceration. The court normally follows these recommendations.

I chose to fly to Miami alone. I held out hope against hope that it would be a probated sentence. My stomach was filled with butterflies, as though I was about to catch the opening kick-off of a football game.

The ornate courtroom Judge King loved to preside in seemed to be vacated of the principal that "Justice should be tempered with mercy." His Honor strolled to the bench, just like a cat would approach a fish wagon. It was March 3rd, 1977.

Philip Kuhn was my appellant attorney. He began with my background as an attorney and my community service. All admirable. How a moment in time would have an everlasting effect on my life. Disbarment and the shame thereof was punishment enough.

Judge King sat impassively. His emotions were impenetrable. He was ready to pounce.

It was now his turn. I took a deep breath, as if expecting a blow to the body. But I would not be prepared for the force with which it was delivered. King agreed with Kuhn's summation. He was convinced that the defendant would never commit another crime. But after all, I had stolen the "good name" of these public officials which had taken them a lifetime to build. Therefore, an example must be made of the defendant as a deterrent to others.

"Billy I. Gray, you will stand. It is ordered and adjudged that, with respect to each of the counts for which you stand convicted, being Counts 1, 2, 3, 5, 6 and 7 of this indictment, that you be committed to the custody of the Attorney General, or his authorized representatives, for a period of eighteen months as to each count. Said sentence to run consecutively. You are advised that you have the right to appeal from the sentence that is herein imposed."

Crestfallen would not begin to describe my feelings. Eighteen months was more than I had expected, but nine years! Unbelievable! My spirit cried out, "Where are You, God? Are You blind that You cannot see, are You deaf that You cannot hear, or are You mute that You cannot speak? Where are You, God?"

I felt like an exposed espionage agent, naked and vulnerable.

Instinctively, fear gripped my thought process. Knowing something about the Belize court system, I knew they did not have an extradition treaty with the U. S. concerning my conviction. Pat could sell our home place and other real estate holdings and we could live a long time on San Pedro. But I could never see my mother again. That was unthinkable; she would die with a broken heart.

The next eighteen months were very difficult. We did our best to live life as normally as possible, but the growing expectation of a prison sentence loomed large in my mind. For whatever reason, Pat and I didn't talk much about it. Perhaps it was the macho man, "I'll take care of everything."

Money was a constant source of worry for me. Income had drastically reduced. No law practice. I made a business deal with Mr. McLarty and one of his associates to buy the majority partnership of the Mayflower franchise for Memphis.

Mr. McLarty's son later become one of Bill Clinton's top advisors. This cured the money problem temporarily. I was in hopes the business would generate enough income in my absence to take care of my family.

Each time the phone rang, my nerves would jingle. Always dreading that one call, "The Fat Lady has sung." It happened on April 13, 1978. The Supreme Court of the United States of America had denied certiorari. Furthermore, I was to surrender to the U. S. Marshall on May 3rd.

That weekend we drove to Ravendon Springs, Arkansas, to tell my precious mother that her son was going to prison. She had always been so proud of me and my career. Her response was gallant and noble. She reasoned God had a purpose in all things, and He would see us through. This was one of the hardest things I'd had to do in my whole life.

The U. S. Marshal, who was a friend of mine, called and asked me to report in the late afternoon of May 3rd. I asked for an additional day, and he granted my request. That night, Pat, Trista and I went to a fine restaurant, ordered the best food and most expensive drinks. I reasoned that it would be a long time before this happened again. I was right.

CHAPTER FOUR

A NEW HOME

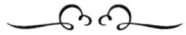

FCI MEMPHIS

There are some people who are natural-born leaders. J.K. was one of those. He was charismatic, with an engaging smile. J.K. could talk a cat off a fish wagon.

He, his brother and son were all serving time for drugs. This was at least the second time J.K. had been sent to prison fro drugs. The Federal District Judges in Memphis were known to be among the toughest-sentencing judges in the Federal Judiciary. But in a tribute to J.K's prowess, in his previous conviction he convinced the judge to give him a light sentence. "I ain't never gonna do this no more, your honor. You can count on me." The judge concurred, and the charlatan prevailed. But not for long. He was now back in prison.

J.K. understood human nature and had a proclivity for taking advantage of people's weaknesses. That included guards as well as inmates. If there was a shortcut, J.K. took it. You could catch J.K. cheating red-handed, and he would convince you it was an honest mistake.

One evening J.K. was shooting pool with some of his cronies. They were loud and obnoxious, as usual. A young man held a pool stick in his hand, watching the other players play. At some point he broke the pool stick, leaving it with a jagged edge. At a moment in time, he took a running start toward J.K. He thrust the stick into J.K.'s stomach and it came out his back.

Horror struck all who were present. Fear gripped J.K.'s face, his skin turned ashen, he fought for oxygen like a fish on dry land. No longer could he rely on his charismatic personality, his cleverness or his subtlety of tongue. It was as though the sun had disappeared from the western sky or a candle had been blown out by a gentle wind, as his eyes closed in death. "For by your words you will be acquitted, and by your words you will be condemned" (Matt. 12:37, NIV).

After we dropped Trista off at school the next day, Pat and I made our way to the Interstate going west to downtown Memphis. Destination — Federal Court House, where the U. S. Marshall awaited.

On the interstate we passed the Mayflower warehouse. Most of the trucks were still on the lot. I prayed that this business would be a success and would support Pat and the children in my absence. I would later discover this was not to be. Due to various circumstances at incarceration, the business was sold to pay its outstanding debts. So much for income while incarcerated. We turned off the interstate onto Front Street, which separated Memphis from the mighty Mississippi River.

Looming on the bluff was the Federal Court House. I kissed Pat goodbye and ascended the stairs without looking back. In the lobby, several people spoke to me, some still calling me "general" from my prosecution days. I rode alone in the elevator to the 9th floor. Getting off the elevator, I was greeted as an old friend by the U. S. Marshall. He led me down a narrow hallway, opened a cell door, and I heard that god-awful sound for the first time: metal against metal.

All alone, I softly began to sing. "What a friend we have in Jesus."

The serenity did not last long. I was escorted in handcuffs to the basement of the Federal Building and put into a car. I was told our destination was the Federal Correctional Institute, which is in the east end of Shelby county. On the way, we stopped at the public hospital to pick up an inmate. A large black man in handcuffs and leg irons was ushered into the car by two armed men. The black man didn't say much. He grunted, and was very hostile to his keepers. He was large enough to be a tackle for the NFL.

When we arrived at FCI Memphis, the structure was ominous. We went through several locked doors before entering the compound. It was an austere setting, cold and harsh. A fence surrounded the compound. On top of the fence was razor-sharp wire that could literally tear you apart.

The prison had five dormitory facilities, an administration building, classrooms and library building, and a gym that also served as the cafeteria. In addition, there was a small building, like a guest house, and this was where I would be warehoused.

Upon my entering, all my civilian clothes were taken. They issued me prison garments that were ill-fitting. The cells were unlike what you see in the movies. They were cement block with steel doors that had a small window so the guards could see you when they had headcount. Bunk beds, up and down, a toilet and a sink.

My cellmate was the big black guy. The guard said he took enough medication to knock a horse out. I was very uncomfortable in his presence.

He told me he had served time in North Carolina. He was on parole and had beaten up two police officers. Of course, his parole was revoked.

I certainly wanted to be his friend, so I started talking to him about God and Jesus. He had been brought up in the church, and therefore responded to this dialogue.

Whenever his medication began to wear off he would sit on the side of the bunk and rock back and forth. These were tense times, as his violent nature would reoccur. Fortunately for me, after one week they sent him back to North Carolina.

I soon learned the routine. Every other day you were let out of your cell for one hour. You could go to a very small recreation yard enclosed by cement walls, or you could take a shower and get two or three books from the very small library. Or all of the above, if you were quick.

This building was used to keep prisoners who were being transferred, or people like me who had not yet been assigned a prison. The original intent for FCI Memphis was to house youthful offenders. However, due to the massive increase in prison population there were already signs that older men were serving their time in this facility.

When you were in the holding cell you could have visitors on most days. When you were in the general population you could have visitors any day. I was never in the visitors' room with my family that there was not a certain medical doctor from Texas in there with his sweet young thing. Of all things, this medical doctor was incarcerated for cattle rustling. Can you believe that?

One day while visiting with Pat and the children, a guard unceremoniously announced, "Gray, you're going to Texarkana tomorrow." We were in shock, as it had been rumored I would be incarcerated at FCI Memphis.

Early the next morning, before daylight, the guard told me to pack my few belongings. He issued me rumpled prison clothing, handcuffed me, put a chain around my waist and leg irons. Here I was, the dangerous criminal, surely a threat to society.

The bus was old and ragged. It was full of inmates, each seat occupied, all smoking. The driver and guard sat behind a wire cage for security purposes.

The inmate who sat in front of me turned and growled, and shouted profanities at me. "The first chance I get I'm going to kill you," he said, for no apparent reason. "Who is this guy," I thought, "and what does he have against me?" I began to silently pray for God's protection.

Across the aisle a man was burning himself with a cigarette and screaming. What in the world was going on? This was like a zoo or an insane asylum.

Soon I found out the bus was not going to Texarkana, but to the Springfield, Illinois prison. This prison not only housed inmates, it was a federal prison hospital, and housed the mentally unbalanced. Suddenly it all made sense, but did not reduce my discomfort level. The guy in front would kill me if he had a chance. I was beginning to understand what real prayer meant.

After a long bus ride, we pulled into the antiquated prison. We shuffled our way into a room where the guards showed the compassion of chain saw killers. We were unshackled and told to strip as a group. The guards proceeded to hose us down with a fire hose, delighting in our discomfort. If this was not humiliating enough, while still wet they covered us with some powder, like baby powder, to rid us of lice or anything else we might be carrying. They gave me a smock and ushered me to a small, dark, one-man cell. No outside light could penetrate these walls. I lay on the bed and cried out to God. What a shameful ordeal — naked in front of other men, hosed down like an animal, de-fleaed like a dog. Scared for my life, and not certain if I was ready for eternity.

I didn't sleep that night, and stayed in constant prayer. What was I doing in Springfield? Was this to be my destination? Could I survive in this environment? For the first time in my life, my skills, knowledge, connections could not come to my rescue. God had me where He wanted me, completely dependent upon Him.

Before daybreak the next morning, a guard banged on my cell door. "Get up, you piece of crap, and get ready for a bus ride." "Where am I going?" "Shut up and get dressed."

Handcuffed and in leg irons, I got on the bus. I sat in the second row, behind a huge white man who had a shock of white hair. These inmates seemed like more normal people. Conversation, laughter, and some seemed to be getting reacquainted after a long absence. I soon learned that was the case, as they had served time together previously.

The big guy in front of me was called "Big Jim." He turned and introduced himself. He had an engaging smile and a nice personality. He had served time before in Texarkana, but he "only" had a five-year sentence this time, and should be out in two years. He knew the system and how to work it. Jim had sung on the Grand Ole Opry. He had ridden a white horse to the town square in a small Georgia town and "run out all the niggers" with a bullwhip. It was as though he was going to a family reunion. Jim would prove to be a very valuable friend.

After many hours, the bus rolled up in front of the prison in Texarkana. The prison was old. Some said it was built at the beginning of WW2 to house war-time prisoners. The current population looked over the new crop of inmates with jaundiced eyes. Which ones had ratted out another defendant in order to receive less time? Who would be an easy mark to take advantage of? Which ones were candidates to be a "girlfriend?"

For those of us who were first-timers, we were on display, just like the monkeys at the zoo. We were finger-printed and a mug shot was taken. I was assigned to Cell Block A dormitory.

It was early June. Summer had arrived in this Texas town, with a vengeance. Even at night the heat barely dipped below

100 degrees. The prison, except the offices, was devoid of air conditioning. The dormitory had bunk beds on each side of the long, narrow room. In the hall, a large, stand-up fan blew, which circulated the hot air.

Being a novice, my bed was on top at the end of the room. An overnight light shone through the bars directly on my bed. Each bed's occupant was given a small, file-like cabinet in which to place personal items. You had to buy your own lock. As I would soon discover, there is no honor among thieves.

After lights out, it was as though you were in a different world. Most inmates smoked, and the smoke filtered through the air. Not all the smoke came from cigarettes. I learned that what had a funny odor to me was actually marijuana. Yes, right there in prison. Some had nightmares and would scream. Others would curse those who had awakened them. Gas from every cavity was frequent, and the place smelled like an outhouse. Fear crawled on my skin like a spider. I could not imagine living like this for nine years.

The next morning I was sent to my counselor to be classified. "Well, Gray, I see you're a hot-shot lawyer. You probably think you know more than most of us. Just remember, we go home at night and you, smart-ass, stay right here with all the other scum bags. We don't have any programs to benefit you, so you might say we will just 'warehouse' you until they let you out."

I was horrified to learn this uneducated, slovenly man who reeked of alcohol would be in charge of my destiny.

Still reeling from the morning's events, I made my way back to the bunk and my locker. The only thing of value that I owned was a new pair of tennis shoes, only worn once. Opening my unlocked locker, to my dismay they were gone. In my heart I cried, "Oh, Lord, how much more can I take?"

That afternoon after "supper," I went to the yard. Some men were pumping iron. Some running. Some playing handball or bocce, and others just milling around. This was the first time I had been to the yard since being incarcerated. One thing was very noticeable: the blacks, the Mexicans and whites did not mix as a general rule. It was a very segregated society.

Against the side of one building, in the shade, I saw a big white man with white hair. There were about 10 people with him, all singing and playing the guitar. Seeing Big Jim felt like a safe harbor.

When I joined the group, as a listener, they played old religious songs and mournful country western tunes. Since I had lost my tennis shows that morning, I wore prison-issued house shoes that looked like elf shoes. Jim said, "Where in the world did you get those god-awful shoes?" I then recounted the story. All the music had stopped. Jim's eyes squinted and had the look of a warrior about to do battle. "You can't trust them nigger bastards. I'll find out who did it and we'll deal with him."

My job was mopping the hallways and the bathrooms. Going to the yard after supper was the highlight of my day. I would walk a couple of miles around the track, and then sit with Jim and his boys.

One day as I joined the group, Jim welcomed me with exuberance. "Well, we know who the dirty little bastard is. A little nigger boy who works in the laundry. Now this is what we're going to do. I have a friend in lockup that's being transferred from Atlanta to another prison. We'll get somebody to start a fight with the nigger, and four or five of us will be witnesses. Then we'll call for the guard and swear the nigger started the fight. Then they will throw him in the hole, and I'll have my friend to kill him. He ain't ever gonna get out anyway, and besides he owes me. That's a humdinger, aint it!"

The esoteric reasoning had my tongue stuck to the roof of my mouth. "You mean you would kill somebody over a pair of tennis shoes?" "Listen, little buddy. If you don't show you are strong in here, you'll end up as somebody's sissy. So what will it be?" My safe harbor didn't seem so safe anymore. Secretly I prayed for God's wisdom. If I said no, that would abrogate the only person who had reached out in friendship to me. On the other hand, my conscience could not tolerate such a senseless killing. "No, Jim, a pair of tennis shoes is not worth the end results." "Okay, little buddy, you are on your own. May God help you." "That's what I'm counting on, Jim."

After a few days, I noticed an inmate who was processed with me was in a two-man cell and didn't have a cellmate. Desperate to get out of the dormitory, I asked my counselor if I could move to that cell.

"Gray, you're dumber than dirt. You don't just move into somebody's cell." How naive I was about the system. The inmate, Tony, had served time before and supposedly was mafioso. Little did I know there were a few inmates that get everything they ask for. Somehow, Tony had me checked out and told the counselor it was okay to move me to his cell. I got my toiletries and moved into Tony's cell.

It wouldn't take long to find out Tony was a big man on campus, although he stood only 5'2". Heretofore, we peons would fetch our clothes out of a barrel in the hallway. They were always wrinkled, and never fit. Pants too big and shirts too small.

One morning, coming back from breakfast, I began to sweep our floor, when Tony walked in. "My cell-mates don't sweep and clean. I have a boy who does that. He sweeps, mops and waxes. And by the way, you need to dress better." Tony always had on brand-new khakis, or freshly-pressed ones.

That night when I came in from the yard, there was a brand-new set of khakis lying on my bed. They were a perfect fit. From then on, every other day I would find new or freshly-pressed prison clothing.

One day Tony asked me why I never went to the commissary. Simple, there was no money in my account. "Tell you what," said Tony. "I'll put money into your account. You spend half the allowance on what you want, and the other half buys what I tell you to." That was certainly agreeable with me.

I soon learned that Tony, who was rich, had cut this deal with many other inmates. Soon we had cases of soft drinks, boxes of candy and other treats and cartons of cigarettes. No one else in Cell Block A would have been allowed to have his own private commissary, only Tony.

I saw first-hand what happened when you crossed Tony and didn't give him his percent. It wasn't pretty.

In my way of thinking, other than being a king pin, I had the best deal going. Applying for a job to work in the recreational yard was not to be. Tony's job was to polish door knobs, but he stayed on the phone running his business interests most of the time. On one occasion, Tony whispered to me, "We're going to get you a job in Records." The next day I was assigned a job in Records. At first their reasons were not obvious to me, but soon it would be apparent.

Many inmates were very macho. For example, they told others they were in prison for robbing a bank and were doing fifteen years, when in fact they stole a welfare check out of a mailbox and were doing two years. Well, the inmate movers and shakers would know immediately that was someone they couldn't trust. Therefore, they needed a trusted ally in Records. That was me. What this did was keep me safe within the black, Mexican and white communities, for they all wanted information.

Little did I know that a major decision was about to be made, in June 1978, in the Texarkana prison. Although praying fervently and in constant Bible study, there was a restlessness in my nature. A call came over the loudspeaker that a chapel service was about to begin. I told Tony that I was going. Tony, a Catholic, said, "Pray for me."

When I got there, Big Jim and some of his boys were playing and singing. The Chaplain preached a simple message and gave an invitation. He asked the question, "Are you sure that you're saved?" The question reverberated in my mind. "Are you sure?" In the free world, while attending revival meetings, the evangelist would ask, "Do you know that you know that you know?" And quite frankly, when I was eight years old I walked the aisle of the church and gave my life to Christ, was this an informed decision? Or the emotions of an eight-year-old boy? That nagging doubt persisted, and pride was a barrier from going forward. Why not tonight? I asked myself. Down the isle to the front and on my knees before God, I confessed my sins, acknowledged Him as my Savior and I committed to make Him the Lord of my life. Furthermore, I made a promise to God: if He ever gave me an opportunity to speak on His behalf, I would be His man.

My new journey started that night, and would be implemented the next day. Hello, walk of faith.

CHAPTER FIVE
MY NEW LIFE

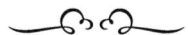

TEXARKANA

There are many interesting people in prison, and consequently many interesting stories. The Mexican lawyer from San Antonio, who ran for governor, is now serving time for drugs. A man who controlled a southern county in Texas who was for years way beyond the law. That is, until the Feds came in. He now was in Texarkana with the rest of us.

One of the saddest stories that I knew of in Texarkana was the conviction of a young man about 18 years old. According to the story, he applied for a loan in Texas for maybe less that $5,000. He defaulted on the loan, and the bank checked his financial statement. They found that he had overestimated his net worth by $1,500. Therefore, the loan had been secured under fraudulent conditions. The young man was sentenced to two years in prison.

Being a young, nice-looking boy, he would naturally be a target for homosexual predators. Trying to cajole and convince this young man this was just part of the prison life did not work. He was resolute in his position of opposition. Now when these perverts have eyes for you, they will chase you down like a dog. If it requires force, so be it.

The young man was placed in a very vulnerable position by a muscle bound bully. As a cornered animal becomes impregnated with fear, so it was with this young man. As the story goes, upon being attacked he, the young man, produced a lethal weapon and sent the bully into eternity.

Thus far not a bad story. But there are consequences for our malfeasance. The young man was taken to court, found guilty and sentenced to 20 years in prison. From 2 years to 20 years, a bitter pill to swallow for defending your honor.

Hope, dreams and desires now dashed, the bloom was off the rose. The flower had faded. A metamorphosis had taken place. A youthful offender had become a mature convict.

"Hope deferred maketh the heart sick, but when the desire cometh, it is a tree of life" (Prov. 13:12, KJV).

Walking out to the yard with Bible in hand was a step of faith. People either didn't notice, or God was protecting me. I made my way to a light pole down the right field line of the softball field. Getting comfortable, I opened my Bible and began to read. "Whatcha doin', Homes?" an inmate asked, whom I didn't know. "No, my name is Gray." Actually, he was saying "homes" as an endearing term meaning "Home Boy." That meant you were accepted more or less like a brother.

His name was Firestone from the hills of West Virginia. According to him, he was 48 and had been in juvenile or prison facilities 35 of those years. Firestone claimed to have been a Pentecostal Minister at one time. He was very inquisitive about scripture, in addition to having some weird interpretations.

The next day, a couple of other fellows joined us at what would become known as the prayer pole. The next day more men came. We would all commiserate, sharing our heartfelt needs. Their concerns were family finances, unfaithful spouses, legal appeals and problems within the institution. At the conclusion I would lift up their prayer requests. Our numbers had reached 18 when the Lord answered one of my prayers.

My counselor said, "Gray, I don't know how you did it, but we are shipping you out to FCI.Memphis." My heart leapt for joy, and I immediately gave God the praise.

Although I now had a good situation in Texarkana, it was not best for the family. It was a very long distance to come and visit. Many of these men were hardened convicts. They had learned to have sexual relations in the visiting room, passing drugs orally, mouth-to-mouth. Although my family did not know what was going on, I had determined they would never be exposed to that behavior.

Saying goodbye to Tony, Firestone and a few others was surprisingly difficult. Early the next morning I was on a crowded bus, and the only passenger going to Memphis. My mind wondered what God had in store for me with my new commitment.

We arrived in Memphis late that night. As I got off the bus, a guard asked me to identify myself. "Gray, this place is too dangerous for you. There are people here who would like to harm you from the days you were a prosecutor." It seemed all the blood in my body fled, and I was limp. Surely God had not brought me this far for no reason. "We think it best that you get back on the bus and go to Maxwell Field in Montgomery, Alabama." He was taken aback when I said, "If you can't protect me, God can and will." "It's your choice," said the guard. "I just hope nothing happens to you on our watch."

They assigned me to a dormitory initially where there was no permanent residents. Unlike Texarkana, the dormitories were just for sleeping and minimal recreation. For all other activities, you had to walk on a sidewalk for at least 100 yards. This was okay unless the weather was inclement. Word got around quickly when new inmates arrived. Unfortunately, my reception would not be treated with warmth.

For the first week I was not allowed to go anywhere outside the dormitory except to eat. You would eat in shifts, a dormitory at a time, to reduce the comingling of inmates.

After a week, the authorities came to the conclusion they had identified those who would do me bodily harm. I was assigned to dorm 5, where I knew no one.

The chapel was a separate little building, large enough for church services and two private offices. One was for the Catholic priest and one for the Protestant minister. This was a very unusual situation in Memphis, as the chaplaincy program was under the auspices of Prison Fellowship. Prison Fellowship is a private Christian organization located in Washington, DC. Its founder is Chuck Colson, former counselor to President Nixon and a former inmate. The program was viewed with a great deal of suspicion from government chaplains as well as correctional officers. Most inmates felt as though chaplains were just an extension of correctional officers. Therefore, an inmate would be reluctant to confide in most chaplains.

Bill Bershears was the Prison Fellowship Chaplain. He was a member of my Free World Church, Germantown Baptist. Consequently, he knew all about me before I arrived. Needless to say, this was an advantage. Bill had set up a program in which the Protestants had a deacon body of five.

Only because I was educated, they (the inmates) immediately thrust me into a leadership role. Looking back, the makeup of the deacons is humorous:

John was a black man from Alabama. John was illiterate, seldom spoke, but loved the Lord. He said he was in prison for mailing a threatening letter to the U. S. Attorney. I never did figure out how an illiterate could do that.

Jerry had spent many years in prison. He at one time dabbled in white magic. Jerry was prone to seizures of depression for long periods. The chaplain thought this was the residual effect of practicing white magic.

Johnny was a small, moody man who loved to sing and play the guitar. A great deal of his life had been spent in prison. He was very dogmatic in his beliefs.

My favorite friend and deacon was Blue. On the outside, Blue was affiliated with a motorcycle gang. His body was strewn with tattoos. He had long blond hair and a beard. Serving time was nothing new for Blue. Some of the atrocities he had committed on the outside do not bear repeating.

Blue's father was a Pentecostal preacher, who would not forgive Blue or accept the fact that he had become a Christian. This hurt Blue very much, for he surely sought his father's approval.

Blue believed the scriptures, where it says, "Compel them to come in." Being a large man and having an even larger reputation, Blue would stand outside the chapel and force some inmates into the chapel.

Then there was me. This constituted the deacon board. Somehow, in God's infinite wisdom, He made it work.

My cellmate was a man named Tom. He was from Louisiana, and a professing Christian. He was active in the chapel programs. At first we had long, theological discussions. Tom was somewhat moody, and his interpretations of the Bible were rather narrow. In spite of our differences, we were amicable cellmates.

FCI Memphis inmates were paradoxical in a sense. Twenty percent of the population was overtly homosexual, while a good percentage were macho, always pumping iron and getting their bodies as hard as rocks. Many times the macho were closet homosexuals. Those who were overt would dress as femininely as possible, and often wear facial makeup.

Contrary to what many free-world people believed about homosexuals, as being weak and sissy, this was not always the case. Many times if you messed with one's man or curried his favor, you could end up dead or badly hurt. On the other hand, some were so feminine, they liked to be dominated and would submit to multiple affairs. The authorities ignored this, even when a gangrape occurred to an unwilling participant.

Chuck Colson came to the prison with several other dignitaries to observe how this pilot program was progressing. People had spoken to him about me. We were introduced, and a friendship began. Everyone thought my sentence was unduly harsh, and Chuck was no exception. Perhaps his interest was because of all the notable politicians who testified at my trial. Perhaps it was because we were both lawyers, and both had served in government, albeit on a far different level. I would like to think it was because we are Christian brothers, and he realized a wrong had been perpetrated and was reaching out in love. When Chuck got back to Washington, he made several appeals on my behalf, yet to no avail. Although disappointed, what I didn't realize was that God was just beginning with me.

After a couple of weeks, I received my permanent assignment. Based on my background, they thought I would make an excellent school teacher. "What am I going to teach?" The counselor gave me a list to choose from. I chose Constitutional Law, Contracts and Business Law. These classes were three days a week for one hour. Much like college. My schedule was Monday, Wednesday and Friday, one class in the morning and the other two back-to-back in the afternoon. Otherwise, there were no other obligations except preparation.

There were two reputed members of the Mafia on this compound. One was from New York and the other from Boston. The New York person was affiliated with a union. He was a roly-poly man with an engaging personality. Supposedly he had something to do with the demolition of an airport construction project.

Jimmy, from Boston, looked like Jeff Chandler, the movie star. Premature grey hair, in excellent physical condition and a demanding presence. I don't recall how many devotees he had, but he was in charge.

When I walked into my first class it was full. Filled with the two guys who had connections and their followers. The surprise on my face must have been apparent. How would they respond to an inmate in charge? Would discipline be a problem? And, if so, who would enforce the rules? The first day was quiet and orderly. Some squirmed in their seats, unaccustomed to an academic setting.

After class, Jimmy came up for a little chat. "Don't worry, all of these boys will behave and not give you a hard time. You see, if they get credits in your classes that will help them with the Parole Board. If there is a problem, let me know."

In my neophyte experience, I was beginning to understand the prison system.

As it turned out, most of the same inmates were in all three of my classes. The head of the Prison Education Department was ecstatic. Part of his job performance was predicated on how many inmates took classes to improve themselves. And all three classes were filled to the brim. He didn't have a clue.

Some of these men were quite bright. Others could barely read and write. Therefore, the subject matters were far too advanced for their intelligence. I quickly learned in giving tests to use multiple choice or True or False. It was easy for the brave to help the hopeless, especially when I had to leave the room.

The Deacon Board decided before Christmas we would like to have a part in sharing with those less fortunate. It was concluded we would help an orphanage that was run by Catholic nuns. All those who attended Bible studies or the Protestant worship services were invited to participate. We could give from our commissary accounts. The idea was approved by the warden. Our chaplain would solicit help from the outside, and the Sisters would give sizes and needs, as well as toys. We never considered the Catholic inmates, because they had their own programs.

One day Jimmy from Boston approached me. "How about the Catholic boys participating in the Christmas party," Jimmy asked. "That'll be great with me," I said, "if the chaplain can get it approved." "No big deal," Jimmy responded. "They don't need to know where the gifts and money come from."

A few days before Christmas, our gifts started arriving and were stored away. The next day, the chaplain asked me over the loudspeaker to come to his office. "Billy, there is a tractor-trailer outside filled with gifts, clothes and toys designated for the orphan children's Christmas party. How in the world did you arrange that?" Needless to say, I was stunned, but had a pretty good idea where they had come from.

The next day another large shipment of gifts came by truck. By now the Administration was aware something was up, and they were furious.

I arranged a clandestine meeting with Jimmy. "Jimmy, what was meant for good is turning out bad. The warden is going to send the second truck back with all those goodies." "Well, I got another tractor-trailer coming from the east," Jimmy said. "Ask the priest if the Sisters can see that others less fortunate in Memphis can use your generous gift." "Consider it done," Jimmy said.

We invited the entire prison population to come to the Christmas party. The little orphans came into the prison scrubbed clean, neatly pressed trousers and dresses, and with smiles that would light up your life. The nuns were gay, exuberant and giddy as school girls. Santa Claus and his helpers arrived with untold bags. Yuletide was heard throughout the chapel and the excitement reverberated like wind chimes during a big blow.

When Santa called each child forth by name, the toys and clothing were just what each wanted. Screams of excitement and tears of joy all rolled up into one word — happiness. After all, we were celebrating the birth of our King.

Even some of the old, hardened cons were touched. Many had to leave, not wanting anyone to see their tears. Some stood afar off, too afraid for their emotions to be tested.

As we stood in a circle, with our heads bowed, thanking God for the gifts and asking God's blessings on the benefactors, I opened my eyes during the prayer. Jimmy looked at me and gave a wink. I concluded there is some good in everybody, and there is truly a God in Heaven.

Time passed slowly in Memphis. I did feel as though I was being warehoused. What good purpose was this serving? For me or society? Spiritual growth continued, and, unbeknown to me, God was preparing me for the next stage of incarceration.

We heard one day that a regional official for the Federal Prison system was on the compound. I was walking to the library and this official and I crossed paths. I stopped and introduced myself to him. He looked at me like I was a piece of dirt. It was inappropriate for an inmate to engage in conversation with such a dignitary.

I stated my case as aphoristically as possible, knowing time was short. God works in strange and benevolent ways. The dignitary actually looked at my case file, and asked the question, "What in the name of sanity is this inmate doing in this prison? Get him to a camp."

Well, the warden and education director didn't want to lose their "star" teacher, and argued against this move. But the sovereign God of the Universe already had aligned the galaxies to transfer number 106-193.

There had been a Federal regulation that if your sentence was for so many years, you had to serve so many years before you could go to the Parole Board. I fell into that category. But, by the Grace of God and a rule change, or perhaps both,

I no longer fell into that category, so during the course of the first year I went before the Parole Board.

Pat was allowed to come into the hearing and be a witness. Even in simple, smart clothes, she appeared ostentatious. It was apparent to the Parole Board we were not the typical sort of incarcerated family. The Parole Board looked at my rather flimsy file. No reports, no disciplinary actions. "You were convicted of one count of Wire Fraud and five counts of Conspiracy." "Yes, sir," I replied. "How much money exchanged hands?" "No money exchanged hands, sir." "And your co-conspirator died before trial?" "Yes, sir." "Then what in the world are you doing with a nine-year sentence? No codefendant, no money. If you didn't have an A sentence which means you will have to serve one-third of your sentence, I would let you go today." Therefore, based on my behavior, I had a preliminary date for parole of April 1981.

Pat and I rejoiced at having a parole date, but two years still seemed like forever. But maybe, just maybe I could go to a camp where they had furloughs. That became high on my prayer priority list.

CHAPTER SIX

MY MENTOR, "THE PREACHER"

It was a grey, overcast fall day. Winter was on the horizon, and wanted a premature birth, as the winds howled and coughed up cold air. As I sat in the prison's law library, looking out, my mood was as somber as the weather. My mind reflected back to better times. The sugar-white beaches, the emerald-green waters of the Gulf of Mexico, romantic strolls on the beach under moonlight, and, oh yes, the voice of a preacher. His voice was pleasant; some might describe it as a voice of velvet. Soothing, charming. His messages were powerful and poignant. At the conclusion of his sermons, an announcer would give the preachers name and church, Dr. James Monroe, First Baptist Church, Fort Walton Beach. I wondered if that preacher would be shocked to hear from a convicted criminal. Nothing to lose, so I decided to write.

The letter was lengthy, and recaptured how I first heard of him, and described in detail the three sermons I had heard him preach. Although I was only in my first year of a nine-year sentence, I wanted to know if his church would accept a former prisoner into the church.

Really not having any measured expectation of an answer to my letter, it was with great joy I received an early reply. Going to my cubbyhole in the library, with nervous hands and a racing heart, I opened the letter.

Dr. Monroe was appreciative of my remarks about his sermons. He further stated his church had a prison ministry. Indeed, being a convicted criminal would not preclude one from being a member of his church. As a matter of fact, one of the deacons was an exinmate. In addition to all the above, on his way to Missouri he would stop by and visit me.

I was overwhelmed with joy.

Time moves slowly in prison. It's like a child waiting for Christmas or a birthday. As the day approached for the visit, every nerve in my body was on pins and needles.

The call came over the loudspeaker. "Inmate Gray, you have a visitor." The visitors waited outside the visitors room until the inmate had been processed and seated. It was up to me to make the first move, as Dr. Monroe would not recognize me.

As the door swung open, a stately-looking man walked in. A commanding presence that had scholarly overtones. Dressed in a brown corduroy suit, his eyes searched for me. I thought he looked a lot like Woodrow Wilson. The guard allowed me to go up and greet him. Have you heard of love at first sight? Well, this was a bonded friendship at first sight. A first step, if you will, that would take us on many new ventures and to other countries.

Almost a year passed, with frequent correspondence. One day out of the blue, I was told that I would be transferred from FCI Memphis to the prison camp at Eglin Air Force Base in Fort Walton Beach, Florida. I was so happy and thrilled that my body could hardly contain my spirit.

When you are transferred to a minimum security camp, they purchase a bus ticket and let you travel alone. The old lawyer mind kicked into gear. I learned that an inmate from

Eglin would pick me up at the bus station in Fort Walton Beach and carry me to the prison to check in. I asked Pat to call Dr. Monroe and see if he could pick me up at the bus station and take me to the prison. He called the warden, and was given the okay.

The plan was risky. It could add years to my sentence. Most assuredly, the time would be served in a lock-down prison. It seemed to be worth the risk.

At the bus station I would check my bag and give the ticket to the driver. Pat would be in the car parked nearby. While people were getting on the bus, I got off and walked to the car. It would take the bus 20 hours to get to Fort Walton Beach, and we could drive there in nine hours, meaning we would have at least ten precious hours to be alone.

The next morning at the appointed time, we met Dr. Monroe at the Waffle House. We ate breakfast; I kissed Pat goodbye. Dr. Monroe and I went to the bus station, picked up my bag and headed for the prison. When we arrived, there was a small entrance on the side of the building where inmates would check in, but Dr. Monroe marched us into the main entrance, through the hall into the warden's office. The warden invited us to sit down, not realizing I was an inmate. When Dr. Monroe introduced me, the warden laughed out loud and said, "I've had governors, judges, state senators, sheriffs, lawyers and doctors, but no one has ever come through that front door but you." I knew I was in the presence of God's man and the Lord's hand was surely on me.

Eglin Federal Prison Camp was my fourth prison. Initially, I was in FCI Memphis, transferred to Springfield, then to Texarkana, and then back to FCI Memphis. Given a parole date, the federal system assigned me to a camp. Generally, the population in a "camp" is reserved for white-collar criminals and snitches.

Memphis had some highlights, as they were trying a new Christian Chaplain procedure. It was run by Prison

Fellowship, Chuck Colson's organization. Although not part of the federal system, it was still highly structured.

EGLIN PRISON CAMP

Many people held lofty positions in the free world before becoming incarcerated. As alluded to previously, at Eglin we had former governors, sheriffs, state senators, and so forth. There also were businessmen worth millions of dollars. You would think a person from that kind of background would emerge as a leader on the compound. Not so.

What does make a leader at a prison camp? Well, we had a leader at Eglin Prison Camp. Joe the Butcher.

Joe was raised in New York, and was reputed to be in the Mafia. He was a short man, maybe 5'4", and weighed over 200 pounds. He was muscle-bound, and hard as a rock. Joe was a butcher by trade and a butcher for hire. He said he used to put lead weight on the scales so he could charge more for his meats.

I never did know what Joe was serving time for, but he had served a lot of time in Atlanta Federal Prison before coming to Eglin. At some point in time, while in Atlanta, Joe became a Christian. The staff thought this was all a ploy for early release. There was such a change in his demeanor, conduct and attitude that the staff could not believe what they were witnessing.

Nevertheless, they continued to observe Joe with a great deal of scrutiny. Soon, even the greatest naysayers, were convinced this was for real.

It is almost unheard of for a prisoner to be transferred from a lock-down penitentiary to a prison camp. But God is still in the miracle business, and Joe found himself on the way to Eglin.

Joe worked in the kitchen. These men would rise early in the morning, but would have the afternoons off. Joe would pump iron each afternoon to keep his body taut. He loved to play softball, and his position was second baseman. He was not the prototypical second baseman, but Joe named it and claimed it.

He was a regular at our 4:30 prayer group. Quiet and observing, soaking up every word like a sponge. Wherever Joe went, many of the inmates from New York would follow: prayer groups, church services, lifting weights or playing softball.

One day at the 4:30 prayer meeting, a discussion ensued about who wrote the Bible. And how do we know that it's accurate after all these years. Most everyone expressed an opinion. I watched Joe as his eyes would cut toward whoever was speaking. They spoke volumes without saying a word. Confusion and anger. When Joe spoke it was like E.F. Hutton speaking. The room became silent, as Joe asked a question. "What do you say, Billy?" "It doesn't make much difference what I say, Joe, but it is what the Bible says, and this is what the Bible says:"

"All scripture is given by inspiration of God, and is profitable for doctrine, for reproof, for correction, for instruction in righteousness" (2 Tim. 3:16, KJV).

Joe said, "Well, that settles it," and a chorus of Amens came from the New York contingency. That question was never raised again.

Well, Joe continued to mature in the Lord and be a quiet influence on the inmate population. The day came when we watched Joe waddle across the line to the free world. We were glad, yet we were sad. It was like when your favorite football player retires. Joe, the Butcher, now standing in the "gap" for God.

"Therefore if any man be in Christ, he is a new creature: old things are passed away; behold, all things are become new" (2 Cor. 5:17, KJV).

But now, at Eglin, this was a different deal. It was a preeminent program patterned by inmates without authoritarian interference. Much of the trust factor had been created by the inmates previous to us and the leadership of Dr. Monroe.

My first assignment, cutting grass in the Florida heat, was no bargain, but soon the chaplain clerk was released from prison and, because I could type, I was given the job.

The chaplain was George Castillo, a native of Belize. Because I had spent several years trying to buy property and obtaining good title in Belize, we became fast friends.

Each day at 4:30, right after the evening meal, we had a prayer meeting. Anywhere from ten to thirty men would attend. We were unsupervised and shared our heartaches, disappointments and joys unabashed.

Generally it was my job to keep the men on course, and close with prayer.

Some of these men were not Christian, but seekers of the truth. A few, but not many, were there to con the staff and perhaps the parole board. However, those who were true born-again believers were novices. Some grew to be very mature Christians.

The demographics of the attendees was very interesting. Former governors, state and local officials, judges, sheriffs, doctors, Hall-of-Fame baseball players, and lots of lawyers and drug dealers. Regardless of your cast in the free world, the holy time was a common denominator. No "big me and little you."

We petitioned the warden to allow us to have an all-inmate service on Thursday nights at 7:00 p.m. Our request was that no prison official attend, and we would monitor ourselves. Much to our amazement, the request was granted.

A new inmate, by the name of J. W. Dawsey, was a Pentecostal preacher. We asked this sweet, high-strung man if he would preach on Thursday nights. Of course he agreed, for this was what he was born to do.

Our first service was announced, and the little chapel overflowed. Some inmates stood on the front steps, and others on the sidewalk. Most had never seen a Pentecostal preacher. He jumped up and down, spit, sputtered, ran down the aisle, and jumped up in the air and clicked his heels. Obviously he would speak in tongues, and some thought the rapture was occurring and others believed he was demon-possessed. The emotional symphony went from sublime to sacred to death. We were all exhausted at the conclusion of the service.

Brother Dawsey came and went. I knew immediately this type of service was far too challenging emotionally for most of the inmates. Dr. Monroe encouraged me to take over the preaching, which I did.

At Eglin there were no walls or gun towers. Only a line that, if you crossed, meant that you would be sent to a place with walls, gun towers and perverts. Believe you me, that's no bargain.

Eglin Prison Camp is located on Eglin Air Force Base property, located in northwest Florida. It is a serene setting with a few amenities such as a softball field and a couple of tennis courts. On the backside of the compound was a small inlet of backwater. With clumps of trees, where outdoor life was served. Birds and squirrels were plenteous, and silence was only seldom broken by a screaming Air Force jet.

Most of the men worked on the Air Force grounds, cutting grass, weeding and raking sand traps. It was hot in the summer and cold in the winter.

I never did understand the mind-set of prison officials. A doctor would be assigned to work the golf course, while an electrician was assigned to medical records.

During working hours, many days I would be the only person in the chapel. This gave me an inordinate amount of time to study, pray and grow spiritually. Other than studying Greek or Hebrew, it was as though I was in seminary.

The occasional furlough gave me some balance in my life, and kept family ties strong.

We had a prison inmate choir. First Baptist Fort Walton Beach would invite us to come on a Sunday night. We would sing a couple of songs like, "I'll Fly Away," and then a testimony. This would be repeated two or three times, and then I would close with a short message. Large crowds would attend these services, and a wonderful reception followed. Other churches began to ask us to come. We struck a bargain with the warden which would allow us to go out once a month. First Baptist and Dr. Monroe were always our favorites.

At Eglin we had phone privileges on our time off and at night before bed check. All long distance calls had to be collect; therefore I called only once a week. One day they paged me in the chapel to come to the Administration Building. There I was told that I needed to call home. In prison you stay in a state of paranoia, so anything and everything that could go wrong came to mind.

When our big house was sold Pat and the children moved into an apartment building in German-town. Pat, although a registered nurse, became a high school teacher. Her eyesight was poor from an allergic reaction to medicine as a child. She was therefore a very slow reader and only became proficient through her tenacity. Being a school teacher was not easy for her and each night she arduously prepared.

One night after the children had gone to bed Pat was working on her school plan for the next day. The evening was pleasant and the sliding glass door was open. She sat on a couch with her back to the sliding glass door. Abruptly someone grabbed her around the throat and began to squeeze. Some how she managed to call out, "Ty help me!" Ty, although not large, knew no fear when it came to protecting his mother. His bedroom was on the second floor. Being a hunter, he fetched a shotgun and bounded down the stairs, yelling, "I am coming mother." The intruder left as quickly as he had come. This is the story I received by phone from Pat. I could tell the event had destroyed her already shaken confidence. Oh, how she needed me at this time and I was AWOL. I shared scriptures with her and prayed but that still did not compensate for the lack of a hug... a pat... a kiss.

One positive thing taken away from this occurrence was that Ty had demonstrated that he took seriously the charge of protecting the womenfolk. Shotgun and all! Beware!

I prayed profusely that God would provide a way for me to help Pat. To encourage her. "Why not ask for a furlough?" my mind asked. Well, the truth of the matter was that it would be 16 months before I was eligible for a furlough. The argument continued in my mind. "Do you believe in scripture? Of course I do. In the Book of James it says, 'You have not because you ask not.'" That settled it for me. Now a plan must be devised and implemented.

In a facility designated as a camp, the head person is called a Superintendent, as opposed to a Warden. Our superintendent was Mr. Quinlan. He was different from most prison officials. He was nattily-dressed, wore horn rimmed glasses, and could have been an Ivy League professor. But not only were his looks and attire different, but his attitude, as well. He had not come up through the prison system as a guard or assistant warden, case worker, or any of those things. He was an attorney for the Federal Prison System in Washington, DC. His ambition was to one day become the head of the Federal Prison System. In order to accomplish this goal, he was required to spend time in the field as an administrator, warden or such. He did not think of all prisoners as scum-bags. Some were decent men who had made a mistake. Knowing this, I devised my plan, bathed in prayer.

I filed a request to see the Superintendent. It was granted. I then made the audacious request that the meeting be held in the chapel rather than his office. When he agreed, I knew God was in control.

No phones, no secretaries, no interruptions, just me, the Super and God. I told the story about what happened to Pat, and how important a brief visit was for her well-being. I appealed to his family ties, as a fellow lawyer, and as a person who claimed to be a Christian. I had argued many cases to a jury, but maybe never as effectively as this.

The verdict came in. Furlough granted.

P.S. Mr. Quinlan became head of the Federal Prison System.

OUR FAVORITE MEMORY

While much of the memories of prison life are not among the most precious for me or my family, there is one that stands out as a precious stone among the gravel of that period of my life.

It is a memory of Christmas that my daughter Trista and I hold most dear to our hearts.

Trista shared these memories with me.

On Christmas Eve in 1979 I was only seven but I can still remember laying in the back seat of the silver Thunderbird after nine hours of driving from Memphis to Fort Walton Beach, Florida. I could see momma's beautiful blonde hair outlining the edges of the front seat and her little hands grasping the steering wheel as she fretted, "Don't run out of gas Betsy, don't run out! We're almost there."

I never knew why she called her car Betsy, it seemed more like a cow's name to me but that is what she called her car. She often spoke to her car as though it were alive and listening to her every command.

I remember watching the street light flash and feeling confident that Betsy could get us over the Brooks Bridge and to the gas station before she ran dry. We coasted into the station on the corner of Okaloosa Island. Momma got out of ol' Betsy dressed in a full-length rabbit fur coat to pump gas. Brr. It was cold. I could see the palm branches blowing in the wind.

As Momma pumped and paid I remember thinking that Santa was already out delivering presents and I wondered if he would bring me that pink stroller and baby doll I asked for.

As excited as this thought was though it couldn't compare with my anticipation of seeing my Poppa, the greatest man alive! It had been a long time since I had seen him. Eglin Prison was 500 miles away from our town home in Memphis. I longed to see him every day. When I saw other little girls playing with their daddys I would feel jealous but then I would stop and think to myself that they didn't seem like they were having near as much fun as me and my Poppa would have together.

Momma quickly got into the car slamming the door shut. "Are we almost there momma?" I asked.

"Yes, Trista, Aqua Villa condos are just down this road." She said through chattering teeth. "Are we staying on the beach?"

"Yes, you will be able to see the Gulf of Mexico from our window."

"What about a Christmas tree, did Poppa get us a Christmas tree?"

"A Christmas tree! How on earth could he do that?"

"I don't know how but Poppa can do anything"

Just then we turned into the condo parking lot. The building was five stories tall and the same color as swimming pool water. We got our suitcases and road the elevator to the top floor. When the doors opened the cold air blowing off the gulf sent chills up and down my spine. The wind howled as it blew down the open hallway. The sky was black as velvet but the stars were bright like rhinestones. I could see the North Star and I thought that's the star that pointed to Jesus and I wondered if it was this cold the night He was born.

Suddenly my attention was on momma who was feverishly trying to get the door open. "Oh no, the door is locked! Jimmy Hale was supposed to leave this door unlocked with a key inside for us." She exclaimed. The thought of having to stay outside a minute longer was nearly unbearable. I turned around and looked at the star again and whispered a prayer to God for help. No sooner did that prayer come out of my mouth than did the neighbors door open up. They enquired as to our situation and then invited us in. Oh how warm it was. She gave me some hot cocoa with marshmallows and let momma use the phone to call Jimmy Hale. Jimmy was knocking at the door before I finished my cocoa. We grabbed our luggage and headed off to our room. I saw that star again and it winked at me. I smiled and winked right back and whispered, "thank you God."

As we walked in the first thing I saw was a Christmas tree. The sweetest little Christmas tree you've ever seen in your life. It sat on a table right in front of the door. It was about two feet tall and had corkboard gingerbread men hanging from the branches with little red berries. "I knew it, I knew Poppa would get us a tree!"

"Well, of course he did Trista," momma said confidently.

Just how had I, Trista's poppa, managed to procure a Christmas tree for his little darling.

It was unusually cold, dark and foreboding for Northwest Florida, in December 1979.

Christmas was rapidly approaching and the mood in Eglin Federal Prison Camp was somber.

Even the Jewish and the very small Muslim population seemed to be affected.

There was virtually no evidence in the camp "Twas the season to be jolly." No Christmas lights, songs of "Joy to the World," no demonstration "It's better to give than to receive."

As I walked the perimeters of the camp the cold wind would come in gushes. Our uniforms were not conducive to warmth in this weather. Uniforms consisted of navy color cotton pants and shirt. If you worked in landscape or other outdoor jobs you were supplied with a cotton windbreaker. Those of us who had clerical jobs were not afforded the windbreakers. The clothing was not adequate for this weather.

The Commandant of Eglin Air Force Base issued an order to the Superintendent of prisons to issue adequate clothing to the men in the field or he would close the prison camp.

The next day a shipment came for the outdoor workers. In addition everyone was given a blanket for their bed as the dormitories were not insulated for this cold weather.

I did not fit into the category of one to receive a jacket. My gray sweatshirt over my blue cotton shirt would have to do. The wind blew my undisciplined hair as my mind raced back to past Christmases.

It seemed so long ago we were having Christmas in the big house. Eight foot Christmas trees, stockings hanging on the hearth, and decorations everywhere. Candles that burned with incenses. The smell of turkey and ham, cookies and candy. Christmas music floated through the air like smoke from a pipe and all was right with the world. The space under the Christmas tree had long been exhausted, no room under the tree. Presents galore, something for everyone. The mood was giddy with high expectations. And just think Santa Claus was yet to come.

The cold rush of wind brought me back to reality. These were different times. No big house, funds depleted, freedom expunged. Even with all the past success the bottom line of the balance sheet was a negative.

In a few days Pat and Trista would make the 500 mile trip to visit me. I had somehow made arrangements for them to have accommodations in a 2 bedroom condo on the Gulf of Mexico. Other than my love that's all I had to give them. For a giver that seemed precious little.

The next day the weather was the same. Many inmates were getting hair cuts to look their best for their visitors over Christmas. In spite of the weather and the grey dull appearance of the camp the spirit of Christmas would crash over the indomitable incarcerate spirits of these men.

One of the hardest things about serving time is the monotony. As I made my way to the chapel to begin my duties as the Chaplin's clerk little did I expect this day to be different.

The Chaplin was from Belize. He came from a very poor family. Excepting the call on his life to the ministry he was educated in the United States and became a prison Chaplin. He was far more than just an extension of the administration, but was truly interested in the spiritual condition of each inmate. As I was very familiar with Belize we formed a great friendship. It was never big I and little u.

As I walked in the chapel that day the Chaplin greeted me with his usual engaging smile and a hearty welcome. "Billy G" as he always called me "How would you like to go to town with me today." My heart leaped with joy as this was unprecedented. An inmate getting to go to town, WOW. "You bet chap," I responded.

The Chaplin checked out a prison pickup truck and we left the camp. It had been so long since I had been in a moving object I almost got motion sick. It was then that the Chaplin told me what our mission was, "We are going to Sears and pick out a Christmas tree." My exhilaration from being out of the prison camp was immediately deflated just like a punctured balloon. There would be no Christmas tree for my 7 year old daughter pity impregnated me like high tide washes away the small sea shells. My ego and pride had been lowered to the abject poverty level.

Sears was located in a mall with other major stores. I watched in amazement the hustle and bustle of the crowd. Christmas music aglow, Santa Claus's HO HO HO reverberated down the walkways. Children standing in line to see the grand old man. Some patient, some fidgety, some brave and some scared.

Families walking hand in hand, bonding and caring for one another.

This was a world I once knew, but that was so long ago.

"How about this one Billy G the Chaplin called out." His voice startled me and brought me back to reality. It was then that I realized my rumpled clothing was not in step with those sartorially attired. No Merry Christmas sweater on me. Just a navy blue cotton shirt and pants issued by the federal prison system. "No chap, that's not big enough and the branches are too spread out. Not a good choice." I look for a tree that if I had a home and not a cell that would be pleasing to the eye. "Now this is what you need." It was a seven foot artificial scotch pine loaded with limbs. The Chaplin agreed and a purchase was made.

I felt good for the Chaplin but bad for myself. As we waited to check out I spotted a small two foot Christmas tree. It was all decorated with balls and lights and ribbons on a perfectly sturdy stand. Do I dare ask? It could mean trouble. What the heck give it a shot. "Chap you know that my wife and daughter are coming down for Christmas." "Yes you have a beautiful family and I'm happy for you." "Well chap you see my daughter is only 7 years old and Christmas is a really big thing for her. I was wondering if maybe that little 2 foot Christmas tree you could buy for me and I could pay you back".

I had been the Chaplin's clerk long enough to tell when he was touched. He was touched, and he made the purchase.

I was already planning my next move unbeknown to the Chaplin. As we loaded the big and the little tree into the bed of the pickup truck the question came up what I would do with the tree.

"Well Chap some friends of mine helped make arrangements for Pat and Trista to stay in the Aqua Villas condominiums during their visit. It's over on Okaloosa Island. If we could, I would like to place the Christmas tree on the dining room table of the condo. It would be such a surprise to my family and it would make my Christmas." The eyes of the Chaplin began to moisten. "It must be hard on you and your family after having so many luxuries of life."

By God's grace the manager was there and the condo vacant. He agreed to let me place the little tree inside. I placed the tree on the dining room table with careful loving hands.

As I looked out the condo window the waves were tumultuous, the wind sharp and cold as a knife but peace and joy had come to the condo, a warmth that is indescribable. I knew a little girl who would be overjoyed with a little, a little recognition, and a lot of love.

When we got back to the prison camp I stood a little taller and there was a quickness in my step. The place didn't seem so dark. Jesus had restored the joy that had been stolen from my heart.

After all isn't this all about Him.

Christmas day had come. The weather was still gloomy and cold. Inmates showered, brushed and cleaned, trying to look their best for a very special visit. Soon the loud speakers would boom out "Inmate so and so you have a visitor." We all anxiously waited for our name to be called.

"Inmate Gray come to the visiting room." My heart leaped with joy. It was like waiting to receive the kick off in a football game. My high expectations however became fraught with fear. Was this too little.

The palm trees swayed with the force of the wind. My confidence dipped as low as the thermometer.

Up the steps through the door and I heard "I knew you would, I knew you would, I knew you would," as the prettiest 7 year old in the whole world rushed toward her poppa. "I told Momma you would have us a tree, I knew you would, I knew you would." I picked her up and held her tight as my body shook with sobs. Pat came to my open arms and the three of us were encircled in a spirit of love.

Pat spoke, "Billy Gray after all these years you never cease to amaze me. Trista was so sure there would be a tree and I thought it would be impossible, but not for my Billy. I'm not going to ask and I don't want to know how it got there unless it was an angel."

About that time Chaplin Castello walked by and I gave him a wink and said to Pat, "It was an angel." Although cold and wintery outside it was warm and balmy on the inside.

CHAPTER SEVEN

COMING HOME

Although, through exercise, I was in very good shape physically, and matured daily spiritually, time wore on me like a collar that was too tight. One day a probation officer came from Pensacola to interview me. He seemed somewhat aloof, and asked mundane questions. "Upon release, how will you earn a living?" "Where will you live?" "Will the community accept you?" "If we decide to let you out on work release, that will depend on the availability of a halfway house in Memphis." "Memphis!" I exclaimed. "I want to live in Fort Walton Beach." My wife and children have already moved here. Both children were already enrolled in the public schools. They were members of First Baptist, and going back to Memphis had never been a consideration. He responded that Florida already had enough criminals on probation and certainly didn't need any more. The interview was concluded, and I was crestfallen. During the Saturday and Sunday visit with Pat, Ty and Trista, much of our conversation centered around my release date. And from there, we would dream our dreams. A condo on the beach; me being a real estate developer; having a prison ministry and me being a member of First Baptist Church. This became a matter of serious prayer for the whole family.

Several weeks went by, and the probation officer summoned me for a visit. With a great deal of trepidation, I made my way to the appointment. "Gray, the State of Florida, for whatever reason, has agreed to let you be paroled in this State. Furthermore, it is our conclusion that you be allowed six months in a halfway house before your final release. This is highly unusual, but all parties concur." I thanked the officer profusely, and told him the Sovereign God of the Universe had heard my plea. "So you really are a Christian," he responded. "So am I." Amen, and Praise the Lord.

When you had a release date, they would post your name on a bulletin board outside the dining hall. Sometimes as early as two to three months before the date of release, there would be your name. A couple of times each day for three months, I would check and make sure my name was still on the list. Each time it was like a shot of adrenalin through my whole body when I read my name.

Although elated, there was much to do at the camp, and much to contemplate upon being released.

I must pick my successor as clerk for the chaplain. He must have typing and administrative skills. By all means he must be a Christian and compatible with the chaplain. Several inmates had already approached me about the coveted position.

As the final days wound down, not only was it time to look ahead, but to look back as well.

What had I learned? One thing God had taught me is that you can't serve two masters. Entrenched into the world system, doting on materialism is not an avenue to God's blessings. My priorities had changed from secular success to spiritual investing. It was quite apparent to me that I would spend the rest of my life involved in God's service.

Most of the men who participated in the Christian program did not come back to prison. This is in stark contrast to the recidivism rate for those who tried to make it on their own. However, there were some professing Christians who disappointed us.

One of the men at FCI Memphis had become so acclimated to the prison system that he could not adjust to the free world.

Then there was Blue, my protector, a hero in a sense, and an outspoken pontificator for the cause of Christ. I learned that Blue had returned to the motorcycle gang, left his family and forsook his beliefs. They found the body of Blue in a ditch. He had been beaten to death with a chain. His corpse lay there for some time before being discovered.

As I looked back, I lamented over the young or weak who were forced into homosexual activities. For those who lived in constant fear. And those who had no hope. If only they knew the King of kings.

But these disappointments paled by comparison to the many victories. Mafia people getting saved. Black and white getting saved. Politicians and plebeians getting saved. He who has ears, let him hear.

The countdown to zero was rapidly approaching. An old, dilapidated house run by the Salvation Army would be my home for the next six months.

We had a big ice cream celebration the eve of my departure. It was open to all the inmates, and most of the 300 came. There were hugs and mixed tears of sadness and joy. Most of us would never see one another again. I was the only Christian mentor whom some had ever known. But with all that in mind, nothing could usurp the excitement of being reunited with my family.

The newspaper wrote an article about me leaving prison. There were a couple of cardboard boxes filled with personal belongings, mostly paperback books. Some of the inmates helped carry the boxes. The paper said it was like an Ivy Leaguer who looked like he should be in a Brooks Brothers suite rather than prison garb followed by an entourage.

We hugged and said goodbye.

I went out the same way I came in, through the front door. My honey was waiting in the silver T-Bird. Our new life was starting. God had given us a new beginning.

EPILOGUE

Upon being released from prison, there was an exhilaration at being free, but some anxiety about how I could support my family. The Salvation Army gave me a wide latitude, understanding that I would be overqualified for most positions available. I was interviewed for a job at KFC for assistant manager. The District Manager said, "I would not hire you because in two or three months you would be a threat for my job." Finally I got a job at J. C. Penney's, part-time, for minimum wage. My first pay check was for $48 for which I was very grateful.

In prison, I had become so spiritually inclined that matters of the world were inconsequential. Not so now. Issues of transportation, health care, education all loomed large. But the Lord always remained faithful and faileth not (*Lam. 3:21-28*).

We, like most families, had our ups and downs. Financial struggles, me wanting to get ahead of God's time table. Although spiritual doors were opening, nagging doubt persisted as to my direction. Sunday School teacher, deacon, pulpit supply speaker, prison ministry and other opportunities did not seem to fill the void.

In 1984, after much resistance, I went on a mission trip to Chandigarh, India with Dr. Monroe. This was totally out of my spiritual experience, but the Indian people stole my heart. International missions were the epiphany that would fill the void.

In 1991, all was right with the world. My business was flourishing. Pat's weight-loss center was doing very well. Ty was married and had a child. Trista had graduated from high school and was now in college. We owned a nice house in a gated community on the golf course. Speaking opportunities were on the rise.

In 1992, the dark clouds of devastation and death struck. Pat was diagnosed with cancer, and went to be with the Lord in less than ninety days.

Pat Gray

Prison nor any other experience had such an impact on me. The one who had stood with me from the Pinnacle to the Abyss and back again ... gone.

But God is faithful. The long, lonely days were filled with a mission trip back to India.

Since then I have been to India 15 times. God has sent me all over the world and blessed me with seeing thousands of people trust Him as their Lord and Savior.

Evangelizing "one on one" in Barbados

Billy Gray Ministries was founded in 1982. Positive results have been seen in Indonesia, France, England, Chile, Brazil, Greece, Rome, Israel, Guadalupe, Barbados, Grenada and other places.

These days, God continues to use and bless me. Three to five mission trips a year occupy much of my time.

**Preaching and teaching in a remote village
in India to the Banjaras**

I still teach Sunday School, revivals, pulpit supply, men's conferences and grief-recovery classes and Prison Ministry. Billy Gray Ministries is also the major supporter of an orphanage in southern India.

When my work on earth is done and they lay me beneath the soil, my benediction should read, "School is out, teacher has gone home."

God Bless You

For more information on Billy Gray Ministries visit my website www.billygrayministries.org

www.BillyGrayMinistries.com
P.O. Box 6202
Destin, FL 32550
850-654-4492

Printed in the United States
132887LV00002B/1/P